I0160401

the
SHUDDER
PULPS

the SHUDDER PULPS

A History of the
WEIRD MENACE MAGAZINES
of the 1930's
by Robert Kenneth Jones

FAX COLLECTOR'S EDITIONS

THE SHUDDER PULPS, by Robert Kenneth Jones, published by FAX Collector's Editions, Inc., Box E, West Linn, Oregon 97068. Text copyright © 1975 by FAX Collector's Editions, Inc. Jacket illustration copyright © 1975 by Michael William Kaluta. Library of Congress Catalog Card Number: 74-82614.

All rights reserved. No part of this book may be reprinted, except for brief passages quoted in reviews, without the written consent of the publisher. Manufactured in the United States of America.

ISBN 13: 978-1-4344-8624-0

ACKNOWLEDGMENTS

The author wishes to express his gratitude to the following:

Rick Minter, for his interest and support from the time some of this material first appeared as a series of articles, and for his later intercession which led directly to this volume.

Walker Martin, another "author's advocate," for the loan of many issues that form an integral part of this study, and more importantly, for his encouragement long before this book was started.

Wyatt Blassingame, an author's author, if ever there was one, for his graciousness, solicitude and responsiveness.

Bernie Wermers, for the many magazines he made available.

Les Mayer, for the loan of magazines.

Art Dobin, for the loan of magazines.

And to two collector-publishers, many thanks: Fred Cook, whose BRONZE SHADOWS precipitated this history, by providing a forum for a briefer version, and Lynn Hickman, whose PULP ERA printed additional supplementary material since integrated here.

Last, but not least, to the following publishers, for their gracious permission to reproduce covers and interior illustrations from material still under copyright.

Popular Publications: for covers and interiors from the following: ACE-HIGH DETECTIVE, DIME DETECTIVE, DIME MYSTERY MAGAZINE, HORROR STORIES, RED STAR MYSTERY, SINISTER STORIES, STRANGE DETECTIVE MYSTERIES, TERROR TALES–copyrighted 1933, 1934, 1935, 1936, 1937, 1938, 1939, 1940, 1941;

copyrights renewed 1961, 1962, 1963, 1964, 1965, 1966, 1967, 1968, 1969.

Popular Library (The Thrilling Group): for covers and interiors from the following: THRILLING MYSTERY--copyrighted 1936, 1937, 1938, 1939, 1940, 1941; copyrights renewed 1964, 1965, 1966, 1967, 1968, 1969.

Also, covers and interiors have been reproduced from the following magazines and dates: ACE MYSTERY, 1936; DETECTIVE SHORT STORIES, 1937, 1938; EERIE MYSTERIES, 1938; EERIE STORIES, 1937; MYSTERY ADVENTURE MAGAZINE, 1936; MYSTERY NOVELS AND SHORT STORIES, 1939, 1940; MYSTERY TALES, 1938, 1939; SHOCK MYSTERY TALES, 1961, 1962; UNCANNY TALES, 1939.

CONTENTS

ILLUSTRATIONS

INTRODUCTION

The pulp magazines of the thirties seem as far removed from the tempo of our times as such contemporaneous period pieces as Marx Brothers comedy routines, MGM musicals, flagpole sitting and big bands. At least, you would think so. Except for a few digest-size science fiction and fantasy publications--a far cry indeed from the earlier lurid cliffhangers--the pulps today are no more. In their place we have pulpstock paperbacks, an ungodly amount of which simply parade pulp vices (and virtues) in a new package.

Gone are the days when an author would write stories of war in the air, even though, as one commented, "I had never been within fifty feet of an airplane," and such other assorted hair-raisers as "a series of pampas thrillers on the basis of reading one travel book, and western thrillers without reading any books." Pulp writers quickly learned one lesson: it was better to know nothing about their subject. Then, facts wouldn't get in the way of the plot.

No longer do struggling word merchants hustle to the editor's office in the morning to grab up a story need, dash back to their red-hot typewriters, and knock off several thousand words of slambang action in time to get back to the editor to pick up their checks before the banks close that afternoon. Writers today generally operate at a saner and slower pace.

Originally, pulps were mass-produced as a cheap thrill for the working man (and schoolboy) eager for light reading of a sensational nature. They were written quickly, to be read the same way, and discarded. No one thought of them as a quality fiction commodity, nor even as an object to save or venerate. But that's not true now. And thus we have an anomaly. Today, pulps have reached an exalted status--reminders of a happier era, perhaps?--along with such other pop cultural products of yesteryear as silent slapstick, old radio shows, and comic books of the thirties and forties. They have become part of our nostalgia heritage, totems of our thrill-fiction past. Collectors now buy, sell, preserve and revere them. And in contrast to the pulps' original audience, these collectors, for the most part, are generally well-educated and well-read.

THE THRILL BOOK, the Clayton ASTOUNDINGS, early DOC SAVAGES and WEIRD TALES, these magazines today command high prices--fifty, one hundred, two hundred times over their original newsstand price. Pulps have acquired a rare-antique prestige. Pulp lovers, like coin collectors unwilling to clean a treasured article for fear of changing its original condition, hesitate to erase marks from their cherished covers, or tape disintegrating magazine spines, for fear of dulling or otherwise disturbing the garish sheen of the illustrations. Some collectors protect their prize possessions with plastic covers, the object of affection only taken out and looked at on special occasions. Others read them, discuss them, analyze them--with a wary eye on how they are handled, of course.

Just what is behind this love affair? It's hard to pick out any one reason. But part of the answer probably has to do with an inherent need, a craving, for stories that tell a story, for pure adventure, unpretentious, non self-analytical. In any case, what was headed for oblivion long ago is still with us. These old soldiers, who fought the battle of the newsstands once upon a time, neither died nor faded away. They were simply pensioned off.

Although most pulp magazines should outlive their owners, they are not in the best of health these days. Pages dry out and become brittle, when exposed to the air and a lack of moisture. The disintegration is slow, in most cases. But it is a continuing process. For that reason, such an archive of printed Americana as the Library of Congress has speeded up its microfilming project in recent years, to preserve its collection of pulp magazines and newspapers. Henceforth, researchers may not be able to check the originals, but they will find a filmed reproduction that easily can be replaced if damaged.

Now, as to this present history. Several years ago, as a labor of love, I wrote a series on the pulps for an amateur publication. I use the word, labor, advisedly. There was little source material on the subject. Surely, it seemed, a multimillion dollar business that catered to popular reading tastes for close to a half century would have left some legacy in the form of commentary, articles, reports, studies. But there was little to find. It was obvious that this "little known and officially unrecognized" field, as the NEW YORK TIMES characterized it, was just that. In fact, during the thirties, the golden age of the pulps, more attention was directed to the dime novels of the nineteenth century, than to the dime magazines of the twentieth.

Since then, the situation hasn't changed much. Several fan publications--fanzines, as they are called--deal with the subject, but of necessity, on a superficial basis, or from a bibliographical standpoint. A few books have appeared. But they offered more a cursory look than a comprehensive examination. Our nostalgia boom seems to be passing the pulps by, from the historical standpoint.

Contrast this state of affairs with the attention the comics are receiving. Histories and collections seem to be coming out every month. The pulps' graphic counterpart for years has enjoyed a more favorable "press."

This book makes no attempt at a detailed analysis. The

material derives from my earlier series, which dealt with the horror-terror types–those that promoted what has been termed "weird menace" stories. However, in covering this phase of the pulps, I found that what applies in one area of pulp publishing, is true of another.

Speaking of lack of source material, even many of the editors and authors still on the scene today who cut their teeth on penny-a-words, remain curiously silent. Many have no interest in dredging up the past. As one author replied, "The times you're speaking of are thirty to thirty-five years ago, and I have always made it a practice to forget the past as promptly as possible and concentrate on the present and future." For others, details of the business have slipped from their memories as irrevocably as pulp titles have disappeared from the newsstands. In answer to specific questions about his company's activities, one publisher replied, "I haven't the faintest notion about that . . ." and "I don't remember why we did that . . ."

On the other hand, many others came up with information, and without it, this book could not have been written. This is a book not only about a particular fiction style, that flourished for some eight years in the thirties, but about the practitioners of an American idiom.

There's little social significance to the stories that form the framework of this study. They were churned out by writers needing a quick sale, marketed by companies seeking a quick profit, and bought by readers demanding a quick escape during the Depression years. That many selections have held up well over the years attests more to the inherent appeal of the fast-moving action formula, than to any calculated attempt on the writer's part to create a lasting testimonial. Yet as one author has said, "I never wrote a story for the pulps that wasn't the best of its kind I could possibly write.

I didn't strive for social content, but the writing was the best I could do."

Our period here, the thirties, produced a greater variety of pulp fiction than at any other time. Just about every kind of subject you can name had its own special showcase then: piracy, sports, super heroes, mystery, adventure, love, western, detective, science fiction, air war, submarine war, land war, supernaturalism, and of course, weird menace. Also, this was the period when the pulp business reached its peak. With the forties, the decline was setting in.

Just what was weird menace? Well, that's what this volume is all about, of course. In essence, it was a form of mystery story in which the villain perpetrated seemingly supernatural deviltries, which were logically explained at the end. Several magazines specialized in this form of presentation at one time or another. Here we have reviewed the weird menace tale from the standpoint of publishers, editors, authors, and stories. Weird menacism unfurled all the appurtenances of mystification: bizarre, seemingly unexplainable deaths, ghost-like creatures, and frightening fiends, in a Gothic setting of dreary houses, dark caves, dank forests, of devil cults and demoniac evildoers, of heroines under dire threat, and heroes pitted against seemingly hopeless odds. The sense of doom hangs heavy over these stories. There is nothing to equal their wild improbability today. Our present fiction may have smoothed some of the rough edges, but in doing so, has thrown out some of the excitement that once kept readers on the edge of their chairs.

the
SHUDDER
PULPS

CHAPTER I. "THE WEIRDEST STORIES EVER TOLD"

All of us were kids just emerged from college and we had the time of our lives putting out pulp books. I think one of the reasons for our own success was the fact that we put so much loving care and attention into publishing every issue of every magazine. The smoothest slick couldn't have had more work applied to it.

--Henry Steeger
THE PULP ERA (May-June, 1967)

The year was 1933. That fall, a wave of mysterious maladies struck many areas of the United States. Soon, it had reached epidemic proportions. As was typical in those days, the pulp magazines were the first public media to report the bizarre occurrences. The green death infected its victims with leprosy. . .the fungus death ate away the skin. . .the rotting death turned faces a sickening green as the afflicted aged a hundred years in a few minutes. . .the marble death, later analyzed as a solution of siliceous salts, hardened cell walls into a stony substance.

Terror fiction had taken a new turn, that would keep the readers' gastric juices bubbling for many years to come. Confined to one publication initially, these ghastly accounts soon spread to many others, much to the morbid fascination of a growing readership. They first appeared in a ten-cent pulp called DIME MYSTERY MAGAZINE, one of a growing chain published by Popular Publications. Three years earlier, the company had set up shop, with Henry Steeger as president and Harold Goldsmith as vice president and treasurer. At his death recently, Goldsmith had been retired for

3

Walter M. Baumhofer did this cover for the November, 1933 **Dime Mystery,** the second of the "weird menace" issues.

several years. Steeger, a native New Yorker, was still at the helm, until he sold his company in late 1972, and at the same address on East 42nd Street in New York City. Such stability is rare in publishing circles. He had earned a bachelor's degree at Princeton in 1925, and got his start in pulps with Dell Publishing Company.

At the time Steeger formed Popular, the pulp climate was changing. Westerns were giving way to detective magazines. Horse operas and frontier stories had dominated the twenties. They remained popular in the thirties, but met stiff competition from other forms. So it wasn't surprising that two of the new company's first four titles were detectives--GANG WORLD and DETECTIVE ACTION. DIME DETECTIVE-- one of the most popular and longest-lasting of the company's titles--came out the following year, that is, 1931. This publication caught on quickly, thanks to such authors as Erle Stanley Gardner, Carroll John Daly and Oscar Schisgall. These and others excelled in crisp action and bizarre situations, such as Ralph Oppenheim's super criminal who delights in sadistically branding his victims, or Frederick C. Davis' phantom killer that stalks a pleasure yacht (both in the September 15, 1933, issue). Writers indulged in some horror, but generally stuck to lurid crimes. The contents followed Steeger's dictum: "A murder mysteriously committed before the eyes of the reader."

He visualized DIME MYSTERY as a companion to DIME DETECTIVE. The first issue followed hard on the heels of this announcement in a 1932 issue of DIME DETECTIVE: "If you can lay one aside before the last clue's been followed up--the last shot fired--we'll eat the back cover!" The new magazine featured a two dollar novel, so-called (usually, a reprint), and two or three short stories, for ten cents. However, the novels proved slow-moving. They failed to attract readers. The format was dull. Soon, it became obvious something had to be done, to rescue the publication, or there was danger of editorial indigestion setting in. Usually, publishers dropped unpopular pulp titles. In this case, Popular tried something different.

William Reusswig's September 15, 1933, cover illustrates Ralph Oppenheim's "Brand of the Beast." Scenes like this, with the heroine in some stage of undress, and being subjected to various indignities, appeared in **Dime Detective**, and were adopted for **Dime Mystery**.

"My inspiration was the Grand Guignol Theater in Paris," Steeger has noted. There, simulated tortures and murders curdled the audience's blood nightly. The whip and garotte were as familiar props at these inquisitional blood-lettings as footlights and stage curtains at a play. So his idea was to translate these three-dimensional depravities to the two-dimensional page. DIME MYSTERY underwent a metamorphosis in its October, 1933 issue. The cover unveiled a gleaming new fright face. It was the first in a pictorial gallery, there and in other publications, of man's inhumanity to woman, with the heroines being pursued down dark corridors, nailed into coffins, whipped, choked, clubbed by cowled fanatics, hunchbacked cretins, gibbering idiots and gnarled seniles, all this taking place, mind you, without mussing up their carefully coiffured hair, or smudging their penciled eyebrows and mascara'd eyes. Good grooming is never out of place.

So much for the outside. Within, more changes were evident. The novel had been fifty-five thousand words or so; now it had shrunk to something like twenty-five thousand, thus opening up space for novelettes of ten- to fifteen-thousand words, and short stories about five-thousand words long. The editor called the new "novels" book-lengthers without the trivialities and slow development of the usual novel. "They have all the plot complications, meat and excitement that readers demand," he stated.

However, it wasn't the physical changes, but rather, the story modifications, that were important. Quite literally, a new type of story had come into being. "Dark Council," the editor's page, defined it this way: "There were good mystery stories and good terror stories appearing in half a hundred different publications long before this magazine ever reached the newsstands. . .but no magazine, to our knowledge, had

Another Baumhofer rendition, this time for the November, 1934 issue. Putting reluctant ladies in caskets and graves seemed to be something of a preoccupation with him.

ever combined these two elements of mystery and terror and devoted its pages exclusively to stories of this one heart-quickening type." Half a hundred was a high count. But the point was, that DIME MYSTERY had come up with something different--a notable achievement in a business noted for its follow-the-leader approach.

Well, then, what was all the fuss about? The best answer is that three distinctive elements had been combined into one unusual presentation. They were Gothicism, sadism and weird menacism. It was this combination that excited the editors apparently more than the readers. Individually, there was nothing new here. Gothicism goes back to the eighteenth century, to Ann Radcliffe's *The Mysteries of Udolpho* and Horace Walpole's *The Castle of Otranto,* the latter, incidentally, an attempt to revive the supernatural themes of seventeenth-century French romance. Literary sadism dates from France's eighteenth-century degenerate genius who gave it its name, the Marquis de Sade, and such works of his as *The 120 Days of Sodom.* Now, for weird menacism. WEIRD TALES for years had been concerned with evil entities, threatening forces, and weird manifestations. Suddenly, though, we get into a new area. The weird menaces that stalked the pages of DIME MYSTERY discharged their duties through seemingly supernatural means. But it was calculated mystification on the author's part. Author Richard Tooker later came up with a concise explanation in AUTHOR & JOURNALIST (June, 1936).

"A fearful menace, apparently due to supernatural agencies, must terrify the characters (and reader, but not the writer) at the start, but the climax must demonstrate convincingly that the menace was natural after all."

It was this stylization that set these stories apart from others appearing elsewhere at the time, as for instance, in WEIRD TALES, where the endings were not logically, or I should say, naturally, explained. And when combined with the other two elements, the weird menace approach can be considered a move in a new direction. Certainly it does now, in retrospect, although at the time, it wasn't spelled out this explicitly. But then, the pulp business moved at such a frenzied pace, there was little time for self-analysis.

Dime Mystery's "new-look" issue, October, 1933, had interior artwork by John Fleming Gould, well known for his black and whites in **The Spider** magazine. The following issue (November) and subsequent issues used Sewell. This Gould drawing illustrates Hugh B. Cave's "The Graveless Dead."

In the beginning, the sadistic element was quite mild. The mysterious nemesis' main responsibility was to terrify the hero and heroine, and only incidentally to threaten them at some point with a few judicious forms of torture. Rogers Terrill, the editor, set forth three basic requirements for the stories: mystery, horror, credibility (although he might have prefaced the last with an "in"). Here is how he defined horror and terror.

"Horror is what a girl would feel if, from a safe distance, she watched the ghoul practice diabolical rites upon a victim. Terror is what the girl would feel if, on a dark night, she heard the steps of the ghoul coming toward her and knew she was marked for the next victim. Mystery is the girl wondering who done it and why."

That does it for the background behind DIME MYSTERY's new look. Now let's see what the result was. In that October issue, Norvell W. Page's "Dance of the Skeletons" led off, followed by novelettes and short stories by Hugh B. Cave and John H. Knox, and others. These two in particular quickly took their place among the most frequently appearing and popular authors of the period. Page's novel was a good thirty thousand words--about half the magazine. He had won the feature spot through a coincidence.

Sometime before, he and a friend were relaxing in a speakeasy. The talk got around to writing. The friend told him, "The editor wants me to cut my sixty-thousand-word novel to thirty-six thousand, and get it in by next Monday. I've only written ten thousand, and I like the plot as it is." This happened, of course, around the time Popular was planning to trim the DIME MYSTERY novel to half its length, in order to jam as many foul deeds as possible in the remaining space.

"Mind if I have a shot at it?" Page asked. "I've never

written for that editor, but I can give him thirty-five-thousand words in a week, if that's what he wants."

As one of the fastest-plotting pulp authors in the business, Page had no trouble meeting the deadline. His "novel" follows a young police trainee who investigates skeletons mysteriously found on the streets. Later, it becomes obvious that people are disappearing, only to reappear later skeletonized, the weird process requiring two hours or less. The murder method involves piranha fish, those vicious South American predators that can strip the flesh from a cow in a matter of minutes.

Page describes how he got his idea, in THE WRITER'S 1935 YEAR BOOK.

"I was looking for some clipping that might suggest horror, that would give me a menace to make the reader's blood run cold. I soon found what I wanted, a typewritten note made after coming home from a motion picture. The movie concerned some lad who had gone up the Amazon for something or other. My note stated that the explorer lowered the carcass of a forty-pound pig into the waters of the river and, forty seconds later, lifted out a clean white skeleton."

The cause, of course, was the cannibal piranha. They are only as large as a man's hand, he went on to explain, and they have large mouths fitted with a row of razor-like teeth top and bottom. Using these fish to convert living men into skeletons, and concealing the method by which it was done, then, became the menace for his story.

Working backwards, Page had decided on the murder method, but he had no motive. So he decided to use it to prevent identification of the victims. In a rather involved bit of reasoning, he settled on an unscrupulous capitalist for his villain, who had fallen on hard times. "He kills off certain captains of industry to make the stock of their companies decline. However, mere murder of these men would not depress the stocks. He must contrive to kill them and make it seem they have merely disappeared. . ." In this way, he would clean up on the stock market, Page noted. It was far-fetched, but ingenious.

Actually, this was fairly mild stuff. Before long, the magazine turned to more grotesque menaces. Within the next year, it brought forth a variety of monsters and fiends only exceeded by the forms of destruction they dealt. There was the Hairless Thing, to provide a label. It had neither nose nor ears. Scaly yellow skin was stretched tight over a triangle of bone. Its eyes were round, lidless and bright as two bits of polished glass. The Torso had no legs; it was half man and half gorilla. The Drooler had a gap for a nose and two heavy folds of dead-white tissue instead of eyes. These were just a few; let me continue. The Goblin's mouth was split from jaw to jaw; its purplish tongue lolled between tiers of yellow teeth. The Black Beast, a gargantuan shape, had blubbery lips, thick, flat nostrils, jagged fangs dripping saliva, and a sickening stench. Leather-Skin looked like parchment, with great angry sores. Here is a typical description:

"Grey-green was the face, with hollow cheeks and lank, lean jaws. The lips were red with blood, as if the teeth they hid had crunched on unmentionable things. But the eyes— dear God, the eyes—were bottomless pits of darkness, from whose stygian depths Death peered and leered."

Wheezing, groaning, slobbering, thumping, slithering, gasping, scratching. . .never were so many afflicted so revoltingly. But sometimes, these monsters were not what they seemed.

A green and scaly thing rises dripping from the depths, to seize its victims with clawlike hands, in "The Pool Where Horror Dwelt," by Richard Race Wallace (December, 1934). It seems a sea beast had once terrorized the isthmus. When the mutilated body of a boy is found, it appears that the legend has come true. For the hero, "with the surf and rolling thunder both hammering at his throbbing temples, it was not easy to cast off the spell of the supernatural." The storm strands the group on the island, leaving them to face a creature "bigger than a man and slimy green." The hero finds its lair, in a cave near a pool. Inside are partly dismembered bodies apparently eaten by the monster. He spies something in the pool--a human head. "The top of the skull had been smashed away and the brain picked out, as if serving as a dainty morsel for the Sea Beast before the real meal began." These stories were always rich in such details.

The nemesis abducts the heroine. The hero bests him after a frantic struggle. And what kind of creature does he find?

"The body, Dix saw, was encased in a waterproof rubberized material, thickly coated with slippery, stinking grease. The claws, razor-sharp, were of fine steel. The top of the head was actually a light aluminum helmet, fitted with airports for normal breathing out of water. However, these ports could be closed instantly, automatically turning on oxygen from the light, encased tank that was the beast's humped back."

The culprit is unmasked as the trustee of the hero's holdings, who would have had to turn a rich estate over to him unless. . .he could drive him mad. So we see here many of the characteristics that would appear in these stories repeatedly: the villain who adopts a weird and frightening disguise, bent on gaining control of rich lands, or an inheritance, or something else he covets. Besides avaricious guardians, other noteworthy scoundrels included embittered inventors, rejected suitors, professors dismissed from their posts, and neglected artists. They often adopted a mysterious device to mask their identities, and carried out horrible and unaccountable murders to mask their motives.

This interior by Amos Sewell is for "The Pool Where Horror Dwelt," **Dime Mystery**, December, 1934. It is similar to the cover illustration, (by Baumhofer) which used almost the same scene. For about a year and a half, **Dime Mystery** covers often depicted one of the stories inside.

Thus, when Mexicans and Indians working a tract are killed, their hearts torn out, the superstitious natives point to small, bare footprints as proof of demons. The menace is found to be an acquaintance of the man who had bought the mineral rights to the land and discovered a rich vein of gold. He had smuggled in pygmies from the Amazon basin to scare everyone away, so he could mine the gold himself.

Many times, the prize coveted by the villain leads to unbelievable skullduggeries. Authors made it a point to resolve the complications, in keeping with Terrill's admonition: No matter how grotesque, there must be a logical explanation. But sometimes, the unravelings came unraveled themselves. Probably, the authors figured that as long as some reason was given, no matter how far-fetched, the motivational amenities were being observed. Thus, in one story, the evildoer, who controls his brother's fortune, keeps the brother sealed in a vault. He lures two claimants to the fortune to his house, with the intention of causing their deaths by seemingly supernatural means, with a witness present so he won't be suspected.

Not only the author, but the editor, too, did his best to convince you that ghost-like deviltries were afoot. Another story was introduced in this fashion: **Bound in the desperate fellowship of fear, the living rushed from Gagetown. They left it, ghastly and desolate, to the dead who leave their coffins at night--who stalk, gaunt-eyed, with grave-clothes flapping, seeking eternally for that which none but they may touch.**

Once more, victims are found with their hearts torn out. Several inhabitants, who had apparently died, return as though miraculously resurrected. Here the fiend is the supposed benefactor of the town. He uses his knowledge of cardiac conditions to revive people who hadn't actually died after all. His motive: to stop a power project that would have dammed and flooded the area, disturbing his research into heart transplants (no less), from his hidden sanctum in the cemetery.

These stories were noted for their atmospheric touches, with the opening usually setting the mood, and a pall of gloom hanging over the events like smog over Los Angeles.

"When I saw that strange clearing for the first time, plunging out from behind the screening evergreens, the hairs at the back of my neck prickled and I was chilled by a sudden inward cold. Perhaps it was the oddly ominous shadow as the sun dropped below Dark Mountain's looming peak; perhaps it was the way our dog, Joseph, with the coat of many colors, growled and cringed against my feet, communicating to me a feeling of something horribly wrong about the place."

Locales were foreboding and oppressive. Among the most popular were caverns and mines, graves, hospitals and sanitariums, and refuges in a storm, such as inns and isolated houses, where dastardly deeds always seemed to be taking place just as the hero and heroine arrived.

Several authors distinguished themselves during the first

year or so of the new DIME MYSTERY, not necessarily by the high quality of their work, although it was frequently skilled, as by the regularity of their appearance. Besides Page, Cave and Knox, they included Arthur Leo Zagat, Wyatt Blassingame, Frederick C. Davis, H. M. Appel, Nat Schachner and G. T. Fleming-Roberts.

Within a year from the time of the changeover, the magazine's covers carried the following legend: *"The Weirdest Stories Ever Told."* Set in quotes, the identification imparted an air of literary stability to the publication, even if the stories themselves didn't.

CHAPTER II. MR. POPULAR VS. THE LITTLE GIANT

If ever there was a formula-bound lot, it's the editors of the slicks. You'll find more variety in the worst pulp magazine than in the best slicks.

Ralph Milne Farley
AUTHOR & JOURNALIST
(October, 1935)

It was one thing to write pulp stories. After all, you only had to read your own, and some authors didn't even bother doing that before sending their stories off. But it was quite another thing to edit pulp stories. The sheer grind of the manuscript mill--wading through story after story, trying to fill magazine after magazine--is one of those untold stories of unsung heroes.

Underpaid and overworked. This cliche characterizes the average pulp editor of the time. Most were young men and women under thirty. Publishers liked young editors. Their enthusiasm and ambition (not to mention their lower financial requirements) compensated for experience in many cases. Their earnings ranged between twenty-five dollars to fifty dollars a week. Most pulp editors gained little financial satisfaction, even less acclaim. Their names rarely appeared on the publications they handled. Their day was long, but their magazine life often was short. They came and went as fast as new pulp titles appeared and disappeared, which was often as much as once a month. There is the story of the new editor who arrived at the office one day, arranged his desk, dictated letters announcing his latest position. . .and said goodbye the next day when he was fired.

16

Every day the editor faced a desk that groaned under the mountain of manuscripts he had to wade through. If he got behind, he could never catch up. He had help, though, from the reader. This functionary, not far above the financial level of the office boy, earned between eighteen and twenty-five dollars a week. Between the two, they polished off several hundred typed manuscript pages a day. Out of these hundreds of thousands of words a month, the editor had to find enough appropriate ones strung together consecutively to fill the magazines he handled. Some editors were in charge of three and four, or even more, magazine titles each month.

One of the most important duties of the editor involved "packaging" his product as attractively as possible for newsstand display. This meant that he wrote the blurbs, or teasers, for the stories, sharpened the story titles, or conjured up new ones, selected the wildest-sounding stories to promote on the covers, and surrounded them there with a scintillation of snappy synonyms guaranteeing thrills and chills awaiting the reader inside. In addition, he reeled off in each issue such a stimulating preview of the next month's offerings, the customer would swoon in a paroxysm of anticipation.

Two editorial directors proved very successful in nurturing the exotic wild strains of their respective companies' pulpwood hothouses: Rogers Terrill, at Popular, and Leo Margulies, at Thrilling, Popular's main competitor in this area. Terrill was described as "big in brains, if not in height." An editor under him once referred to him as "a driving man. He would get an idea and hammer at it."

Before coming to Popular, Terrill had worked for T. T. Scott's Fiction House as managing editor of WINGS, ACTION STORIES, FIGHT STORIES and eight or nine other magazine titles. He had also written fiction and articles. When the company suspended operations for a few years, he left.

He was in his early thirties at the time he made the change. He remained with Popular through the forties, then left to become a literary agent. He died in the mid-sixties.

An author who knew him personally, Wyatt Blassingame, has called him one of the finest editors he ever worked with. Others likewise swore by him, for his story criticisms and helpful directions. He hated plagiarism, and wasn't above going out of his way to make his feelings known. This event happened several years after the period under consideration here. The pulp business produced more than its share of corner-cutters. One time, an author sent in a story that Terrill recognized as one he himself had written fifteen years earlier. It was nearly the same, word for word. Apparently the author didn't realize who the editor was. Terrill wrote to the man, praising the story and saying he would like to meet him. The author came to New York and visited the company. He left Terrill's office practically on his hands and knees.

Soon after Terrill helped establish DIME MYSTERY as a weird menace type, Popular readied a new thrill pulp as a companion publication. Only this one would sell for fifteen cents, probably to indicate even better quality. The new title was TERROR TALES, and it was soon obvious that there was little difference between the fifteen center and the ten center. The first issue, dated September, 1934, spread the following gospel:

"Did you ever as a child watch, fascinated by fear, as the shadows in your night-darkened room took on shape and form and furtive, blood-chilling motion? Have you ever choked back a scream of blind, unreasoning terror at the sudden sharp crunch of a footfall behind you on some deserted walk? If you've undergone either of these experiences, you'll remember the quickened beating of your heart, the swifter, tingling flow of blood through your veins.

A few of the **Horrors** and **Terrors,** such as this one, September, 1935, had covers that illustrated one of the stories (in this case, "Death Calls From the Madhouse," by Hugh B. Cave). Credit here is given to John Newton Howett, while the same artist appears on the corresponding issue of **Terror Tales,** with his last name spelled Howitt. It seems **Horror** spelled it one way, **Terror** another, before it finally became Howett for good. Such mistakes, usually in authors' names, now and then crept into these publications.

"That quickened beating of the heart. . .the bodily tension, the peculiarly breathless feeling of unusual awareness, all are part of nature's defensive machinery. . .

"But today, in a generation protected and coddled by the artificial safeguards of civilization, the average citizen finds scant play for those tonic bodily reflexes which are so largely caused by primitive fear.

"Thrills, we believe, fill an important, necessary function in any normal, healthy human life. It is the hope and aim of this magazine to counteract to some extent--vicariously but none the less poignantly--the regrettable lack of this age-old stimulus in present-day life. . ."

This was the "vicarious-thrill theme" that appeared over and over in these magazines. The point of it was that you must read such stories, if you expected to stay healthy.

Permit me to cite just a few more editorial observations the magazine carried on other occasions:

"A queer thing, this fear emotion! Brave men can come through bloody battle untouched by any craven weakness, yet turn pale and shiver in their beds at the distant baying of some jackal dog beneath the midnight moon. . .Fear is also stimulating. . .Fear, the most dreaded of all human emotions, is also the most sought after. . .This magazine is presenting tales which satisfy a primitive, age-old urge in the heart of every red-blooded human--the keen desire to know fear. . ."

This kind of rationalizing was all well and good. But it filled more of a subsidiary role in "selling" the magazine. Much more important were the attention-grabbers: the cover, interior illustrations, titles and accompanying story prefaces. They claimed more editorial attention than the stories themselves. The titles had to be eye-catching; many were reworked by the editor just for that purpose. Often, an author didn't recognize his own piece from the new title. Certain favorite words were used, such as daughter, mistress, wives, fiancée, girl. The idea was to pair them with the likes of Satan, the devil, hell, madman, death, ghouls, plague. The more the title connoted an illicit relationship--which the mystery-terror stories never fulfilled--the better. The result of these match-ups came out as "Mother of Monsters," "Satan's Hand-maiden," "Girl of the Goat-God," "Bride of the Sun God," "Her Suitor From Hell," "Honeymoon in Hell," "Mistress of the Damned," "Death's Frozen Brides." This policy obviously paid off since other magazines were quick to adopt it.

From **Terror Tales,** September, 1935, this Sewell picture for Norvell Page's unusual "Accursed Thirst" shows the artist's ability at rendering shrinking maidens and glowering, threatening villains (in this case, the hero turning into a werewolf).

Once past the title, you came upon the story synopsis, in which the editor was expected to display a virtuoso talent at evoking a feeling of oppressive malignancy.

Here are four examples:

- But the quiet village she had known was now a grim place where terror stalked--and death peered in with hungry eyes on sleeping victims. Whence the townspeople had fled, leaving those mindless creatures to roam at will through its dusty streets and darkened houses, seeking--seeking with their age-old lust for human flesh and blood.

- A tale of a greedy swamp and a bleak house where horror reigned! Of a hideous, man-eating Thing whose soul belonged to Satan --and the dark terrors that it wrought.

- Hungry and blood-thirsting, the age-old Beast of the Swamp had sucked Janet Randall's sister into the cold maw of the marsh, a warm, screaming victim.

- The grey-green specter came from darkness, to force young William Arnold's clutching fingers about the white throat of his own beloved bride. Had he become indeed a bloodthirsting madman--or did the very fiends of hell possess his soul and body?

There was a danger here, though. If the editor wasn't careful (or rather, too careful) he might make the preamble more exciting than the story itself. However, the authors were usually up to satisfying the most "blood-thirsty" reader.

While the stories dealt in gory situations, the illustrations suggested horrible happenings, but avoided bloodshed. It's puzzling why the line was drawn here, since later, other publications didn't stint on graphic gore. For several years, Amos Sewell handled the interior illustrations for Popular's weird pulps. Wyatt Blassingame tells how he would be in Terrill's office when the editor was phoning Sewell. "I don't know if he ever read any of the stories after they were published, but I know he rarely, if ever, saw them before he illustrated them. Rogers would describe the picture he wanted, giving him the work for an entire magazine at one time." Sewell went on to bigger things, such as THE SATURDAY EVENING POST, as did Blassingame. Sewell was very adept at eliciting an aura of malevolency in his renditions of menaced maidens and heroes straining at their bonds. Other interior artists were David Berger, Paul Orban (also appearing in DOC SAVAGE and THE SHADOW) and Ralph Carlson.

Popular's most prolific weird-menace cover artist was John Newton Howett (earlier spelled Howitt), who also painted covers for OPERATOR #5 and THE SPIDER. Walter M. Baumhofer, DOC SAVAGE's cover delineator, provided the DIME MYSTERY covers until 1936, when Tom Lovell took over for a year and a half. Baumhofer's girls had a smartness that early Howett's lacked. But by 1936, Howett's ladies were lovelier to look at, after shedding their maiden-aunt demeanor.

With two mystery-terror pulps under its belt, Popular hitched up its pants for a third serving. HORROR STORIES appeared in January 1935. Like TERROR TALES it appeared with a fifteen-cent price tag and considerable fanfare.

> *With this issue Horror Stories takes its bow--to chill and thrill the thousands who have long asked for and awaited such a magazine.*

Here is a scene from Arthur Leo Zagat's "Crawling Madness," done by Howett in March, 1935, complete with shrinking maiden, leering evildoer, and creeping fear-figures.

Apparently, the "thousands" were not readers of the other two magazines. Again, the stories were similar to those already appearing, written by authors familiar to the readers.

Before long the material appearing in the three magazines became known as "Terrill Tales." As a counterpart to DIME MYSTERY's "The Weirdest Stories Ever Told," TERROR TALES was billed as "The Magazine of Eerie Fiction!" and HORROR STORIES as "Stories That Thrill and Chill!"

During this time, Terrill's responsibilities were growing. Soon, he would become editorial director of some fourteen pulps, and earning one hundred and twenty-five dollars a week. Several editors worked under him, who occasionally appeared in print themselves. Henry Treat Sperry edited DIME MYSTERY for a time, with Leon Byrne as associate editor. Both died in 1939. Loring "Dusty" Dowst--who wrote fiction with his wife, Peggy--served as an associate editor on the three publications. In recent years, he held a senior editorial job with HOLIDAY, when published by Curtis.

Meanwhile, several blocks away, Ned Pines, publisher, and his editor, the indefatigable Leo Margulies, were getting ready to launch their own shudder pulp. The company put out what was known as the Thrilling group of pulps, so called from the many titles preceded by that word. Officially, the company started as Standard Publications, then became Beacon Publications and later Better Publications.

Pines was born in 1905, and attended Columbia University. He started in pulp publishing with three titles: THRILLING DETECTIVE, THRILLING LOVE and THRILLING ADVENTURES. (His brother, incidentally, Robert A. Pines, published COLLEGE HUMOR.) Within eight years, Pines listed some twenty-five titles, many capitalizing on the word, Thrilling. He and Margulies had been friends before the company was started.

Margulies had worked as an office boy for Bob Davis, called the dean of editors, who directed Munsey's magazines. It was Davis who convinced him to quit Columbia and get some practical experience, and Margulies avers he was never sorry. He did research for Fox Film Corporation, and served a stint with Tower Magazines. Pines brought him to Thrilling in the early thirties. The two worked closely together getting the company going. Margulies insisted on certain specific standards.

"We can lick this racket, Ned," he said, "by buying damn good stories, but we've got to pay on acceptance, and I really mean on acceptance."

He had a sharp editorial eye for salable material. A case in point is Frank Gruber. After being turned down everywhere, Gruber took his Human Encyclopedia stories to Margulies. He looked them over and suggested a character change. That was just the ticket to make them sell. Soon, they were so popular, Selznick Studios bought the movie rights and hired the author at a good salary.

Arthur J. Burks has called Margulies "one of the people I shall remember to the last of my days." Earl Wilson referred to him as "The Little Giant of the Pulps," and stated that he made it a point to read or at least become familiar with every story the company bought. Commenting on this recently, Margulies admits that later, he didn't read everything. "I tried to, but that was a mistake." In his book, The Pulp Jungle, Frank Gruber characterizes Margulies in this way:

"Leo Margulies was a short man, not over five feet five. He was a dynamic, forceful man with a low boiling point. . . Several years later Leo took a course from Dale Carnegie and as a result his personality changed. He remained the aggressive business type, but his angry tirades became a thing of the past."

It was in October, 1935 that Pines brought out his weird-menace pulp, using--you guessed it--the word, Thrilling. According to Margulies, "We had seen the success of some other magazines, like HORROR STORIES and TERROR TALES. It was the only type we didn't have at the time; that's why we started THRILLING MYSTERY. For purposes of postal information, Harvey Burns was listed as editor. But you know, that was a house name. We never used real names. I didn't even have mine on any magazine. Another house name was C. K. M. Scanlon. The initials were for my wife. You know, because Henry Kuttner wrote under that name didn't mean he was the only one; others used it too. In those days we had a fiction factory. I grouped the magazines and gave them to the guys who worked for me."

The initial issue announcement was more recondite, if romantic, than what we've seen already:

You who have heard the whispers of Tambihu-I-Naga, the Awakener of Serpents, who have worshipped at the temple of

Mahadevi, the Great Goddess, and have hearkened to the edicts of Durga the Unapproachable!

All of this you have done subconsciously; you have attended the ancient rites that our ancestors knew so well. Suddenly you have found yourself shivering with dread, or thrilling with fear for no apparent cause--civilization's dark background of horror and torture and weird magic has enveloped you. THRILLING MYSTERY is the perfect magazine to fulfill your longing for thrills, mystic experiences and glamorous, exotic settings.

So, although THRILLING MYSTERY copied other magazines on the scene, there was certainly nothing familiar about its editorial commentary. In fact, it was downright incomprehensible (besides being ungrammatical). I guess the arcane names were bandied about to pique the customer's curiosity and make him plunk down his dime to satisfy it.

At the time of THRILLING MYSTERY's debut, the company listed some twelve publications, six using the word, Thrilling, and all under Margulies' stewardship. Within a year, he would be editing twenty or so titles, and earning twenty-five thousand dollars a year, one of the highest-paid pulp editors of the time.

Trade journals in those days carried statements by Margulies regarding the new publication on various occasions. Thus, he listed these specific requirements at one point: material should center around (a) vampires, witches, ghouls, werewolves; (b) strange cults, with demon-god figures; (c) horrible monsters; (d) villains who use horror methods to drive their victims mad.

Later, a more detailed explanation noted, "The woman interest is definitely desirable in the novelette length, although not necessary in the short story. . .Effective are stories in which the weird trappings are employed to scare people away from a locale. . .so that the victimizer can obtain gold, oil or other fortune." Another acceptable plot, he said, was the theme wherein a dying man or offended mystic curses the characters, the villain then committing the crimes and blaming them on the power of the curse.

Much of that sounds familiar, doesn't it? Finally, here's one further directive from Margulies, to highlight a typical situation that proved the backbone of so many weird menace stories. It echoes Richard Tooker's.

"Take one or more human beings who are likable and understandable. Have him or them terrifically menaced by some eerie force. Be sure that a great personal fear is engendered, that life, limb and love are at stake and that the menace is someone unknown to the hero, but that it is someone in the story against whom suspicion is not at first directed." Next, we'll see how TM used these themes.

Margulies is still active today in pulp publishing, with his own company. He puts out MIKE SHAYNE, ZANE GREY, and the revived WEIRD TALES.

Another Howett cover, for November, 1934, proves that the heroine never had a chance. Escaping the clutches of one frightening apparition, she runs smack into another.

CHAPTER III. SECRET SHRINES OF MYSTERY

> *There just ain't very much that's any good*
> *in any medium at any time, and there is just*
> *as good a chance that there is some lasting*
> *gold in them there hills of pulps as in the*
> *mountains of other kinds of publications.*
> John D. MacDonald
> BRONZE SHADOWS (November, 1966)

You might say that Popular and Thrilling operated a writers' exchange, during the thirties. Names like Arthur J. Burks, John H. Knox, Wyatt Blassingame, Paul Ernst, Ray Cummings, Hugh B. Cave, G. T. Fleming-Roberts, and Wayne Rogers appeared under one company's imprint one month, and the other the next, or sometimes, under both at the same time. And of course, these weren't their only outlets, not by a long shot. They were like any pulp authors depending on writing for a livelihood--they had to make sales to as many sources as possible to survive. Indeed, they can be described as spreading themselves thin by laying it on thick.

However, as far as Thrilling was concerned, sharing of talent didn't extend to joint title tenancy. Popular rushed a fourth terror pulp to the stands in April, 1935, with the title, THRILLING MYSTERIES. The use of Thrilling on the magazine galled Ned Pines, who felt that it was practically his own private word. He pressed the point. The two companies settled out of court, with the Thrilling name conceded to Pines. The cause of the disturbance lasted but the one issue. Then of course, six months later, Pines came out with THRILLING MYSTERY.

Worshippers at the **Secret Shrines of Mystery**, as the initial issue of THRILLING MYSTERY was designated, found there some top-flight practitioners of the literary black arts. Besides the names already mentioned, there were Richard Tooker, who also functioned as a literary critic, O. M. Cabral, Hal K. Wells, Carl Jacobi, Joe Archibald, Jack D'Arcy, Jack Williamson, Frank Belknap Long and Robert E. Howard. Several had made their mark earlier in WEIRD TALES. Within a year, the magazine regularly included stories by Henry Kuttner, soon to become one of the most versatile and imaginative writers in the fantasy-science fiction genre. He adopted the circumscribed method of the weird menace approach. That was unfortunate. Several of his pieces started off auspiciously, as seeming fantasies. But they quickly reverted to the accepted style, with the usual explanation of how the villain mystified everyone, and this wasn't his forte.

THRILLING MYSTERY's fiction stayed away from sexual innuendo to a great extent. Oh, there were a few allusions here and there to gently swelling breasts, and eyes gazing lasciviously at tender charms. But that was about as far as things went, in that direction. Nor were the titles suggestive. They ran more along these lines: "The Terrible God," "Devil at the Wheel," "The Dead and the Damned," "Blood in the Night," "The Flame Demon," "The Dude Ranch Horror," "The Yellow Curse," "Spawn of the Slime," "Coffin for the Living," or "The Death Kiss."

To show how circumspect the magazine's approach was, it pointedly avoided two popular stylizations that had been appearing in such literature elsewhere: (1) the heroine "offering" herself to the villain to save the hero, and (2) the hero's love for the heroine jeopardized by the introduction of an evil seductress. These complications provided a pungent touch. But THRILLING MYSTERY seldom employed them.

In fact, although the editor expressed a preference for woman interest in the material, often the heroine played no more than a subordinate role. More often than not, she was not even the main focus of the villain's dreadful designs.

The magazine's covers, however, showed no reluctance in exploiting her. The cover standard had already been set, with the helpless heroine at the mercy of the leering fiend. Thrilling made no attempt to alter this. However, THRILLING MYSTERY's fair maidens generally remained modestly clothed, even though elsewhere at this time, the heroines were getting nuder and nuder. The best that Thrilling offered was a rent here or there at a strategic part of the body, but nothing much to bring a wicked gleam to the eye. The *mise en scène* was gruesome enough, though, with the principals in the arms of skeletons, being stabbed by cowled sadists, flung into burning pits and forced under guillotines. Unlike Popular's covers, Thrilling's showed bloody acts, involving mutilated limbs and headless torsos. In some cases, the inside black and whites were even more sanguine. Interior illustrators included Monroe Eisenberg, Leo Morey, Alex Schomburg, Parkhurst, Jayem Wilcox and Rudolph Belarski, who also painted some of the covers.

Leo Margulies tells how he liked to have a story for every cover of THRILLING MYSTERY (even though he didn't, in every case). "Rarely did we have a story early enough to illustrate. We had about seventeen good guys in the office. When a cover came in, I'd hang it up on the wall and let them look at it, and then have someone sit down and write a story about it." These "cover stories" were invariably very short, easy to dash off quickly. They were actually nothing more than an explanation of what the artist depicted, with the author's byline naturally, a house name. In a few cases, someone's actual name appeared, as for instance, the Mort

Several nonweird menace publications, such as this detective-oriented effort (August, 1935), featured mystery-terror fiction as at least part of their contents. Hugh B. Cave's "Death Stalks the Night" treats of flesh bubbling "horribly in the stew." This poor rendition is by J. W. Scott.

Weisinger three-pager, "Coffin for the Living" (August, 1936), written to order for the dramatic moment in which the hero strains at his bonds as a steel-helmeted, red-suited villain prepares to electrify the heroine in a silver casket-like roaster.

We've already seen some examples of story promotion in Popular. You'll recall that they hinted at deeds so foul and frightening, there was positively no way the stories could justify them. And sometimes they didn't. But in any case, they made for lively reading. The editor-in-charge-of-story-blurbs for Thrilling attacked the problem with equal ardor.

He adopted a slightly different technique. Instead of a paragraph précis, he utilized a sort of headline declamation--bold-face type, in an alliterative arrangement, braced with exclamations. Here is how some sounded.

**A Satanic Spirit Spreads Havoc in an Unholy
Campaign of Destruction!**

**The Virus of Idiocy Was in That Vile Potion Clutched
In a Dead Man's Hand**

**Madness Rules a Crypt of Corruption Where Dead Mouths
Are Sated With Dripping Flesh!**

**A Cry of Anguish in the Fog-Choked Darkness Brings
Ann Flannery to a Scene of Ghastly Evil**

**A Greed-Crazed Maniac Sets the Stage
For a Horrifying Orgy of Human Sacrifice**

**From the Well of Silence Comes the Mocking Laughter
Of a Loathsome Lord of Evil**

**Was it a Witch's Curse That Conjured Up
The Grinning Hosts of Pandemonium?**

And that shining example of redundancy:

**In His Greed for Wealth, a Killer
Creates Terror Through Exotic Forces of Horror!**

Browsing through these lines was not necessarily more fun than wading through the stories--although they may have been better read--but as pulp graffiti, they had a quality so grotesque as to be charming. Who's to say they weren't as important as the cover in "selling" the magazine?

By the time this pulp hit its stride, that is, around the middle of 1936, the whole Gothic framework was undergoing a subtle restructuring. The turgid prose was becoming snappier, less circuitous. Now, such arch-Gothicizers as Arthur Leo Zagat, Nat Schachner and Francis James, practically fixtures earlier in Popular's pulps, looked out of place. They were hardly ever seen in THRILLING MYSTERY, which played down Gothicism.

Sometimes, Thrilling opened the mausoleum to let out a noxious vapor or dolorous lament.

> *Elfin dusk had shrouded the hairpin windings of that spruce-gloomed trail through the Michigan timber country. It seemed hours since we had left the station, yet the driver hadn't spoken once. The mute murk of his lumpy body, hunched over the steering wheel, irked me with a panicky impulse to shout at him, shake him--anything to break the maddening silence of our twisted pilgrimage to the house whose damned secret gnawed in my brain like a yogi's curse.*

More often than not, though, the opening stayed fairly matter-of-fact and to-the-point.

> *Robert Wayne stood gazing down at Hannah Blake, lying so still and white in her coffin. Death, he reflected, had not softened her features. If anything, it had intensified the look of utter ruthlessness she had worn throughout life.*

Like authors the world over, Thrilling's contributors recognized the need for a strong opening to set the mood. They could rise to effective imagery, on occasion.

> *No wind, no moon, no stars. Night knelt
> to earth like a nun, blotting out the heavens
> with her cowl of cold, grey mist. To the girl
> who stood in front of the iron gate, this was
> something like that corridor between this
> earth and the next. The mist was death's
> grey veil.*

From the magazine's own description of itself as a vehicle for "mystic experiences and glamorous, exotic settings," you would have thought that THRILLING MYSTERY would be concentrating on such WEIRD TALES-type exemplifications as, for instance, Lovecraft's erudite elaborations of other races, strange myths and distortions in time and space, or Robert E. Howard's romantic sword and sorcery sagas. Practically nothing along these lines appeared.

Nor did it fulfill some of its other criteria. Remember the four main categories of subject matter given earlier? They were vampires and other wordly creatures; strange cults; horrible monsters; villains who use horror methods. Of these plot devices, the last three only were found. I don't know why supernaturalism drew editorial attention, since very little concerned with the powers of darkness saw the light of day. Maybe the authors simply stuck to the weird menace conventions, since that was a style easy to adapt to, thanks to its set pattern and procedure.

As for the recurring themes, let me give a quick rundown of some respective manifestations.

Cults–A band of Satanists worship at an altar as they prepare a human sacrifice. The Druid ceremony involves an attempt by a madman to heal his wife of leprosy through invoking ancient magic. (It proves ineffective.) In another story, a hunchback captures victims in a specially prepared quicksand pit. They then become the entree for his perverted appetite, as he indulges in Obhelii, a form of African tribal cannibalism.

Monsters–No, there seemed no place in THRILLING MYSTERY for the likes of the Hairless Thing, the Drooler and the Goblin. Instead, a giant ape sometimes was the fear-figure, trained to grab victims for his master. Or someone might turn into a monster, such as the puny private secretary who takes a drug and becomes a powerful, inflamed creature capable of wrenching the heads from the bodies of unfortunates through brute strength.

Villains and Horror Methods --This is the same old story again. There were only so many possibilities; traditionally, the evil-doer was the friend of the family, or even family member, the person least suspected. Among their methods: a pathgenic virus that causes acute polio, twisting its victims into humped, lumpish shapes; a parasitic, greenish tendril-like web that clogs up the nose and throat; and echoing Norvell Page's earlier effort, piranha fish used to create fleshless bodies.

It looks like this lass isn't long for this world, on the March, 1936 cover. Cowled fiends were favorite cover menaces.

Authors delighted in itemizing every struggle and recording every groan of their victims. What they lacked in subtlety, they made up for in ghastly regurgitations. Or at least, that's one way of looking at it.

"A dull black cushion pillowed the awful hair. All the various hues of decay were in the bloated, poisonous-looking flesh, varying from a slimy grey to a dried blue-black. Corrupted flesh had sloughed away from portions of the throat, and in a blackened hollow beneath the chin a white grub had found a home. . .He forced the blade of his knife between the dead, blue lips. I heard a grating sound as he forced the jaws apart. In the cavity that had been the mouth I saw dull, black teeth; one tooth had fallen from its socket and lay upon the blue, bloated tongue. Tangora opened the flask and poured the entire contents down the throat until the mouth was filled to overflowing."

It's easy to see how some of these blood-curdlers would sour the stomach. For extreme examples, two stories by Wayne Rogers were as sordid as any. In "Dance and Die" (July, 1936) a band of thrill-hungry old men cater to their debased desires by torturing young women. The ringleader uses the orgies to get rich by charging exorbitant fees.

"Wildly she struggled to keep on her feet, though the fierce heat was burning right through the thin slippers she wore. Again she was down--and the smell of scorched, burning flesh came up to Larry sickeningly."

There are additional gruesome details, but you get the idea. Actually, this story was unusual for THRILLING MYSTERY, not because of the abhorrent events, but rather, due to the fact that so much attention was paid to torturing girls. More typical of the magazine's emphasis was Rogers' "Hell's Brew" (January, 1936), a vile mixture, consisting of mutilated corpses, a big, black beast (apparently a werewolf)

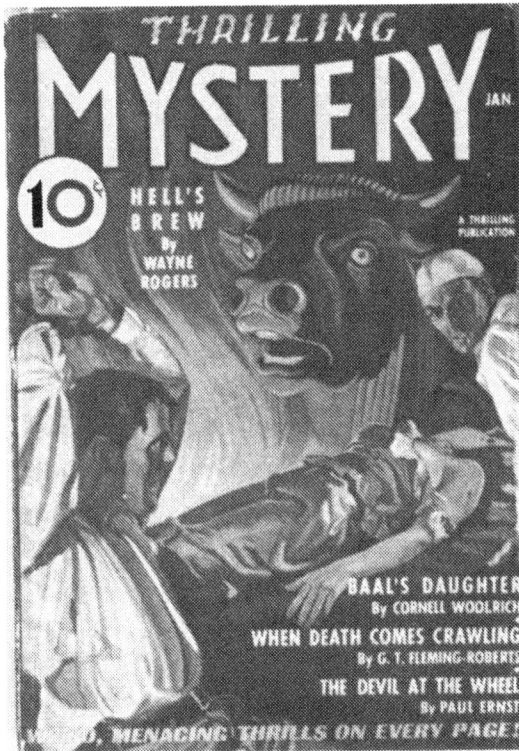

Unlike **Horror** and **Terror**, **Thrilling Mystery** made no bones about showing gory goings-on, as represented by this headless woman on the cover of the January, 1936 issue.

and a fantastic ritual for shrinking heads.

The members of an exclusive club are being mysteriously killed. Investigating, the hero comes upon a hidden room, where he spies what appear to be dolls. The bodies are clay, but the heads. . .

"The head was only a quarter of its actual life size, but Horton identified it without a single doubt. . .Dazedly, Horton turned to the next figure--and flinched from what he knew he would find there. In the shrunken features he recognized another deceased member of the Windsor Club!. . . There were more than two dozen of those fantastically horrible dolls, he noticed--all the Windsor members who had died during the past ten years."

He looks in a large cauldron over a fire pit and sees something bobbing in the thick, scummy, bubbling liquid. It's a boneless, almost shapeless, human head, shrunken drastically. The villain is the surviving member of the club. Obviously demented, he murdered the other members for the hell's brew–the oil–found on the property the club owned, and at the same time, collected a unique doll display.

Let me hasten to point out that many stories took a different approach to such carnage. There was even a villain who apologized, if you can imagine that. As he expires, he explains his actions regretfully. " 'I can't die like this, Ed. I've got to tell someone! I wanted the other farmers to lose their crops, and then they'd have to buy from me to fill their contracts . . . I've been a fool, Ed, a terrible fool . . . ' "

Paul Ernst was one who didn't believe in excessive violence. His "The Devil at the Wheel" (January, 1936) emphasizes bafflement, rather than bloodshed. Passengers on a bus find themselves captives, as their vehicle becomes a juggernaut hurtling through the dark to an unknown destination. Swaying and lurching, it jounces down a steep incline. Later, a splash is heard and a faint, distant roaring, like that of a rapids.

" 'It's no earthly river,' moaned the old woman. 'It's the River Styx. Death driving us–to the land of the dead–' "

They reach their destination and look out on a weird scene. In the flickering, reddish light dance and cavort a score or more of figures that seem to be human–but are so hideously misshapen and deformed that they would have been less horrifying if they had been beasts. They carry the passengers off. Flames shoot up through holes in the rock floor. Satan himself is seen on a throne.

After some harmless prodding and pricking from his "imps," the group escapes in the bus. The whole thing, of course, was a put-on. The villain wanted the property for its natural gas and oil, so he decided to scare everyone away. He didn't even indulge in one modest murder to achieve his ends. In fact, you couldn't be afraid of him if you tried. He was described as "a shaking, babbling man whose emaciated form was quivering."

Admittedly, the ending is weak. But earlier, the dramatic intensity didn't let up, as the terrified passengers hurtled toward an unknown fate. Despite occasional letdowns, many of the stories had similar gripping moments. Some of the scenes were genuinely scary. The writer, Will McMorrow, commented in a letter to the NEW YORK TIMES around this time that "People read woodpulp because they find it interesting. There it is. The mystery is solved." In the case of this and similar publications, it could be added that they also found it exciting. The fear and thrill of the unknown come through strongly in the following.

"The match burned low and seared his fingers. Hastily, he lit another. Then as he stood there, holding that tiny inadequate light in his hand, he felt a cold snake of terror crawl along his spine. Wings of panic beat in his brain. . .For directly opposite him the lid of a coffin was rising. The rotted, dust-covered wood made an odd creaking sound as it moved, a sound like the off-key note struck on a ghostly violin.

"Then as it lifted higher, Lane saw the hand that was moving it. It was a grey and bony hand with long prehensile fingers. Tightly they grasped the edge of the coffin lid and thrust it upward.

"Then an arm appeared, a tenuous, naked arm like the ashen tentacle of some fiendish octopus. Lane's eyes dropped from the ghastly sight for a moment and focused upon the tarnished nameplate of the coffin. Then as the words engraved there registered on his mind, a white madness froze his nerves.

"For the man who was rising from the tomb had been dead for over a hundred years!"

What does it matter, really, that once more, the whole thing is calculated mystification, later to be explained rationally? Well, maybe it does matter, but nevertheless, these were spine-tingling moments.

Here someone is about to slice his own throat, in a typical shudder scene. This one is from "Blood for Kali," by G. T. Fleming-Roberts, in the October, 1936 issue of **Thrilling Mystery**.

CHAPTER IV. BLOOD BROTHERS

The early pulps have a historical interest
for the magazine journalist, for they en-
couraged many new writers.
Roland E. Wolseley
UNDERSTANDING MAGAZINES

Word rates weren't going up. But the opportunities for getting a story published were on the rise, with the appearance of THRILLING MYSTERY, soon to be followed by other similar pulp vehicles. Before long, in fact, weird menacism took on the aspect of a boom. There was no problem in meeting story quotas, though. If there's one truism about the pulps, it's that the demand never outstripped the supply. Authors were up to any production challenge.

We've met Hugh B. Cave, Arthur Leo Zagat, Wyatt Blassingame and John H. Knox. But it was a brief introduction. These four "blood brothers" turned out, between them, some three million pulp words a year, or enough to keep three to four magazines a month going. Let's see how they operated and what they produced.

Hugh Cave (now there's a name for a mystery writer) has been described as a master of the livid phrase. He larded his narratives with such expressions as "agony-mist," "corpse-creature," "retching face," and "shrieking heap." His tales built up slowly and suspensefully to a final harrowing scene. He proved adept at this, although he modestly explains that he "just plugged away, trying to learn how to write by writing."

41

He was born in England and grew up in New England. He started writing fiction in high school in Brookline, Massachusetts, in the early twenties. "At that time I was severely afflicted with the embryonic author's usual desire to do the Great American Novel," he notes. After college, he edited trade journals and worked for a book publishing company. His sales to magazines picked up, so he began free-lancing. He wrote out of Rhode Island, sticking pretty much to himself. "I hardly ever met an editor or another writer," he says.

"From the pulps I moved into the slicks, doing a lot of work for the SATURDAY EVENING POST, REDBOOK, COUNTRY GENTLEMAN and some of the others. And I wrote books, fifteen in all. I'm still writing for the slicks and still doing books. Meanwhile, one of my travel books--about Jamaica--resulted in my buying a famous old coffee plantation in Jamaica's Blue Mountains, and I spend much of my time there now, trying to restore it. Home base has been moved from Rhode Island to Florida. Along the way, I spent some time in the Pacific as a war correspondent, and several years in Haiti." That's Hugh Cave talking today.

Going back to his pulp career, he could be found in some fifty or so publications in the thirties. At the time, he spoke highly of the kind of terror tales he and others were marketing. "If classics were being discovered today, which unfortunately they aren't, a good deal of the discovering would take place there."

A heading for one of Cave's stories in DIME MYSTERY, "Dark Slaughter" (January, 1934) went like this:

> **It was Hope, the young and beautiful wife of Paul Thorburn, who first sensed the frightful lure which called from Black Pond. Later, when the living dead sang miserably beneath a clouded, swamp-land moon, she fought with fear-wet brow to hold her slipping sanity!**

Even the author, himself, would have been hard put to improve on this come-on. With a feeling akin to Poe's "William Wilson," Cave's story chronicles the career of a college student, gaining substance by covering several years of his life. Like Poe's leading character, Cave's hero falls victim to his own base emotions. The plot is somewhat involved. Briefly, it has to do with a visit by the hero and his wife to see his brother. The latter is strangely afflicted, prey to a Haitian drug administered by a student acquaintance of the hero's. The villain was trying to create zombie-like slaves to aid in mysterious researches.

At one point, the two principals are making a surreptitious investigation. They are on a dark stairway when iron bars drop down to separate them:

"Suddenly, my wife whispered fearfully, 'Paul! Someone is coming!'

"I stood rigid. Hope had turned and was staring like a trapped thing into the well of gloom below her. Down there in darkness someone was approaching. The shf-shf of plodding, mechanical feet was distinctly audible."

If it wasn't shuffling feet mounting dark stairs, it was bony hands opening crumbling coffins. For sheer menace and a sense of implacable doom, "The Corpse-Maker," in DIME MYSTERY (November, 1933), rates among Cave's best. In its setting--a sinister retreat--and its mood--mounting danger as a fiendish menace prepares to do his worst--the story compares favorably with "Murgunstruum," a Cave "classic" from STRANGE TALES a few years earlier. Instead of smirking, self-assured vampires skulking in dark corners, a leprous, white sadist (masked to hide his identity) prowls decaying corridors. He is a criminal who was horribly disfigured when making his escape from prison. From his subterranean hideaway, he directs the murders of the jurors who convicted him. They are brought to him to be tortured to death.

The hero, an amateur adventurer and ex-district attorney, infiltrates the lair to rescue the heroine, who was one of the jurors. In these early weird menace examples, the heroes more often than not were private detectives and investigator types, a carryover from the previous detective phase. Later, the emphasis was on "average" guys, caught up in the evil machinations of the villains. The secret headquarters proves a foreboding place.

"The ray of light preceded him, disclosing narrow doors on either side, some of them open and inviting inspection of the rooms beyond. The rooms were empty, dark and soundless as the corridor itself, giving up no secrets.

"The corridor was endless. Its ceiling hung low, suggesting midnight chambers and black vaults in the upper reaches, far above. The walls were cracked, scarred, hurling fantastic shapes into the flashlight's glare. The floor was grit-caked, strewn with refuse."

The hero is captured and forced to watch as the judge who sentenced the villain is strapped into a chair which is then slowly heated electrically. He knows that will be his fate. It was stories like these that the editor said provided "crepitant chills."

Cave's equal in adjectival lugubriousness was Arthur Leo Zagat. In fact, this master of the tortured phrase out-Gothicized just about everyone else. You couldn't help but admire his colorful expressions, even if you did cringe at his idea anemia. He spiced his stories liberally with such concoctions as "choking fetor," "spectral something," "lambent gloom," "virulent torchglow." Most of these authors could turn ROGET'S THESAURUS upside down when it came to atmospheric embellishments. In Zagat's case, he took it apart, page by page. To Roger Howard Norton, a fellow author, Zagat was the "magister trismegistus of the macabre."

Zagat was born in New York City in 1896. He spent his writing days in the city, and died there when he suffered a heart attack in 1949. Here was an author who had been productive so long, that it comes as a shock to learn that at the time of his death, he was only fifty-three.

Zagat's first appearance in print was in a humor column, of all things, in a weekly paper at New York's City College. From time to time he tried his hand at verse. He served overseas during World War I with the AEF's Signal Corps, remaining to study in Paris. He came back in 1919, later married, then earned a law degree in 1929 at Fordham University. So with experience and a good education, he was ready for his professional career: pulp writing. He worked at several jobs, then found himself out on the streets, thanks to the Depression. He was down to $2.41.

He asked his wife what he should do. "You used to write pretty well," she said. "I hear the magazines are paying for stories. There are paper and pencils, and I can borrow a typewriter." From such inauspicious beginnings are literary careers forged.

Hitting the typewriter keys beat pounding the pavements, so he got to work. His first story sold. It didn't take him long to establish himself. In the weird menace genre, he specialized in the longer story, that is, twenty-thousand words or more, what the editors euphemistically termed "feature-length novels." Zagat has been called one of the first of the electric typewriter boys, "wearing his machine (and himself) out regularly." He wrote all kinds of fiction. Two or three of his "novels" in as many magazines might appear the same month, in addition to several short stories. His mystery and detective output was prodigious. Also, he became familiar to science fiction readers. For many years, his Doc Turner series was an attraction of THE SPIDER MAGAZINE. The Red Finger spy stories were a feature of OPERATOR #5.

Zagat and Popular Publications hit it off from the start. His stories were a mainstay in HORROR STORIES, TERROR TALES and DIME MYSTERY, as well as several other titles. Blassingame recalls this incident. "I once went to Rogers Terrill's office and asked him if Arthur Leo Zagat was a real name, saying it sounded too much like a phony name made up for the terror-type pulps. Rogers burst into laughter and said it was a real name and that not more than five minutes before I came in, Zagat had been in asking if Blassingame was a real name because it sounded. . .etc."

To Zagat, story ideas were everywhere. One time he passed the home of a recluse, protected by an electrically charged fence. The mystery intrigued him. What went on there? Naturally, it had to be something sinister. He explained it all in a subsequent story. It was the home of an eccentric inventor, you see. At night, a black, formless killer would roam the grounds, striking down his victims with a death ray.

This Baumhofer cover for **Dime Detective's** November, 1935 issue could have been for any weird menace magazine, since there's nothing to indicate detection in it. The story it illustrates, Norbert Davis' "The Devil's Scalpel," likewise, has nothing to do with detectives, with the hero a medical student.

In his penchant for adapting to his literary uses whatever was at hand, he even turned an operation into an article. During 1935 he suffered a near fatal attack of pneumonia-- probably the only interruption other than eating and sleeping to a twenty-year writing splurge. The setback slowed his pace by two or three stories, but boosted it by one article. The description of his ordeal, in TERROR TALES, reads like one of his chillers.

"During that recent attack, the surgeons bored into my back some nine times with hollow needles from four to six inches long and an eighth inch in diameter. They didn't use any anesthetic, but I had to ask whether the plaguey things were in there. . .Once I got a real thrill when the doctor said, conversationally, 'I'm scraping the sac around your heart, the pericardium.' That was the time they found the bag of pus for which they were looking and pumped infected matter out of my chest for forty-five minutes."

This leads to an amusing comment. Zagat had been so prolific and had been appearing with such undiminished frequency, the editor felt obliged to notify his readers about this temporary halt to his feverish creative pace. He promised more of the author's "brilliant eerie tales" in the near future. But the readers were not even aware of this setback, since a check of the magazines shows that his stories continued to appear uninterruptedly during this time. Undoubtedly, the editor had on hand several manuscripts from this one-man fiction factory, which carried him through.

By the forties, Zagat had become one of the highest paid pulp authors living. Describing his own technique at that time, he pointed to the opening as the most important part of a story. It set the direction for what followed. He liked to interject an air of mystery or menace in the first paragraphs. Often, he didn't know himself how it would be resolved. "I very rarely know the end of my tale when I begin it. I very rarely know the why and the how and the who until I am very near the end of the tale. Most often I am as surprised as I hope my readers will be, as they must be, because I could not have tipped my hand" (WRITER'S 1943 YEAR BOOK).

Let's glance at some of his beginnings from his earlier weird menace days. Here are three examples.

- Laura Standish blurted out her husband's name before she was fully awake. "Frank!" But there was no answer. Even before she realized just what it was that had awakened her, a chill, little quiver of dread brushed her spine.

- Ann Travers awoke with a start. She lifted her head from the rough tweed of Bob's overcoat shoulder and looked dazedly around. The roadster's motor still thrummed the monotonous song that seldom had been out of her ears in the long week since they had left New York. . .Yet Ann was uneasy, oppressed, aware of a creeping chill in her bones that matched the anomalous chill of the desert night.

- The night it all happened we were feeling pretty high in the hut that Jim Hawks and I had made out of wood scrap and old tomato cans.

From the above, it can be seen that since the beginnings didn't actually spell out any direct happening, the author could take off in any direction it suited him. Another aspect that becomes apparent here is that the story is told from the female viewpoint. Zagat used this approach often in his terror tales. It could have been effective. For some reason, he

Arthur Leo Zagat's "House of Living Death" in the first issue of **Terror Tales** (September, 1934) was an auspicious lead-off introduction to a new pulp. That's Shang spiriting away the heroine, while the hero obviously won't be able to do much about it yet.

couldn't pull it off--which didn't stop him from trying. So the result was a tedious recital of the heroine's every apprehensive thought and feeling. This brief excerpt is typical.

"It was barely a hundred yards to the summit of the rise, yet it was an endless journey as within her fear shrieked, 'Look out! Danger ahead! If those men could not fight it, how can you hope to? Turn back. Turn back before it is too late!' Thus fear. And love answered, 'Go on! Go on! At whatever peril to yourself, you must go on!' "

Once started on this tack, Zagat would keep it up for the rest of the story. The result would be a two-page happening told in twenty pages. When he employed the masculine approach, he was much better. A fine effort of his led off the first issue of TERROR TALES. The opening, as usual, sets the mood, for his "House of Living Death."

"Are you sane? Are you certain there is no taint in your blood, no lurking bomb of madness in your heritage that may not explode under sudden stress and make of you a staring-eyed lunatic--seething, perhaps, with the passion to see red blood spurting from arteries, severed by your knife?"

Speaking is Harold Armour, who is railroaded into a private sanitarium. The account is so well put together, you know that on this occasion, certainly, the author knew from his first sentence where he was going. Armour comes up against the giggling, sadistic Doctor Helming, who runs the sanitarium. A guard named Rand keeps the inmates cowed with a blood-spattered whip. The femme fatale, a popular figure in these stories, is seen in the person of Irma Kahn, followed slavishly by her mindless giant of a pet, Shang. And the hero's fiancée, Nan Holmes, like him, is trapped there. All the weird menace gimmicks are effectively employed. The scene with the inmates running amok, Shang lunging about trying to stop them, as the building goes up in flames, and Armour and Nan struggling to find a way out, is one of Zagat's most exciting climactic moments. A disturbing thought at the end hearkens back to the introduction.

"So, as it turned out, I was not insane. At least not insane enough to be committed to a madhouse. Nor, I will admit, are you. But are you sure, dead sure, that you will never be?

"Think about it tonight, when all the lights are out and you stare into a darkness where a faceless something may be lurking, its curved claws reaching noiselessly for your throat."

Wyatt Rainey Blassingame was born in Demopolis, Alabama, in 1909. After graduating from the University of Alabama in 1930, where his penchant for traveling earned him the nickname, Hobo, he hit the road. He got a job on a newspaper, but within a year, was out of a job due to the Depression. Finally, he arrived by a roundabout route in New York City in 1933, with just $2.22 in his pocket. There his brother, Lurton, operated (and still does) an authors' agency. One day Count Blassingame, as Arthur Burks called Lurton, showed Wyatt some pulp magazines.

"These are buying copy. Go to your room, study them, and start writing stories just like these." It was the first time Wyatt had become aware of the pulps. Six weeks later, he sold his first piece of fiction. It was a mystery-terror yarn, a type that stood him in good stead through the years. Before long, he was appearing regularly. Once, just to see if he could, he set out to sell to each of the pulp categories, such as sports, romance, detective, western, etc. The only one he missed, he says, was the confession field. During the thirties, he sold an estimated four hundred or so stories, to some fifty different publications.

He served as an officer in the Naval air service, during World War II. Out of this came material for several hardbound books. In the forties, he made the jump from pulps to slicks, to THE SATURDAY EVENING POST, COLLIERS, REDBOOK and others. At present, he has to his credit a total of thirty-five juvenile books. Occasionally, he writes a magazine article, usually a travel piece. Today, Blassingame lives in Florida and teaches creative writing at a junior college.

Most full-time pulp authors went about their business with a single-minded purposefulness. They didn't have time to indulge in such diversions as sitting around with kindred spirits to discuss life and literature. Or, they didn't have the inclination to stop and explain what they were doing when they were so busy doing it in the first place. But Blassingame was among the few who took time off from writing stories to write about them. (Of course, this brought in money, too.) In one of his articles in a trade journal, he explained the two main plot complications he followed in some form or another in his weird menace work.

1. A character flees from a menace. He tries in every way possible to escape. But the menace overtakes him. When all seems lost, the hero overcomes his adversary.

2. The hero and heroine are trapped at night in a room. Every side represents some dimly seen, mystifying danger. The walls start to close in. The hero has to find a way out.

He would vary these devices from story to story. Thus, "Three Hours to Live," in DIME MYSTERY (October, 1934) follows number one literally, until the end. Then the hero is saved, not through his own efforts, but by a friend. The story is in the form of a manuscript, found in Roger Longfield's hotel room in Montgomery, Alabama. From the hero's certainty of his own fate at the beginning, and an editorial emendation, it appears he will be killed shortly, in some unfathomable way. An old crone had cursed the Longworth family. Soon, the members die, one by one, apparently victims of the curse. Each death is preceded by a bump, bump, bump in the darkened room where it occurred. First the grandfather, then the father, finally, it's the son's turn. He's convinced he can't escape his fate, but flees anyway. The menace overtakes him at the hotel. The final section is an agonized soliloquy, as the doom draws near.

"It'll be here soon. I want to run, to jump out of this chair, dash down the corridor, burst out the door, go rushing down the street where there are lights and crowds. But it wouldn't save me. And I couldn't do it anyway. I'm afraid. . .

"Oh God! It's here! It's in the hall now. The steps. Heavy, slow. Why doesn't it hurry?

"It's at the door, coming in . . ."

The last of the manuscript is written by the hero's friend, who had hidden nearby and was able to unmask the nemesis as the uncle. The murderer had employed a poison-tipped folding cane--which made the bumping sound--to kill off the family members for their money, which he needed to pay off some debts.

There it comes, the mysterious smoke from the coffin; the next thing you know, the corpse will be sitting up, in Wyatt Blassingame's "Three Hours to Live." This is in the October, 1934 **Dime Mystery**.

Another DIME MYSTERY story, "The Black Pit" (June, 1934), written under Blassingame's pseudonym, William B. Rainey, illustrates his second edict. On a dare, a man visits a bleak, deserted house that had frightened him as a child. He must spend the night there. He learns that a homicidal maniac has escaped in the vicinity. He meets a girl, who, it develops, had been hired by his friends to play ghost and frighten him. Needless to say, the lunatic arrives to frighten them both. The couple hide in a room where the flooring ends abruptly over a sheer drop. The insane killer batters at the door to get in. They crawl on a plank over the chasm to a space against the further wall, then drop the plank down. The maniac enters, finds another plank, and swings it across the gulf at them, forcing them to seek protection in a fireplace.

He leaves. Soon, a noise is heard overhead, as the demented man starts clambering down the chimney to get at them. The hero strikes a package of matches and flings them into his face, then manages to push him over the edge to save himself and the girl.

It was shortly after starting his writing career, that Blassingame was approached by an editor at Popular to do a novel-length feature to be called "Operator #5." He was just beginning to earn what passed for a living then, and the thought of a book-lengther a month, pre-sold, made his mouth water. He went home immediately and sketched out a plot. After a few changes, he wrote the story. As he tells it, "The life of the country hung by a thread all the time. But nothing happened that would appear in the papers."

However, when the manuscript was taken into Henry Steeger, he had already had a cover painted. "It showed the White House being blown sky high--an incident that simply could not have been worked into the story," Blassingame ruefully notes. So the series went to another author--

Frederick C. Davis. That was the only book-length story Blassingame wrote for the pulps, and it never sold. "At the time, I was getting one cent a word," he recalls. "Popular raised me to one and a quarter cents a word, which in the course of time, I suppose, repaid me for the work."

In John Knox, we find one of the most versatile and consistently competent craftsmen of the period. Born in New Mexico, he grew up in the South and Southwest. He neglected his studies to write continued stories in old notebooks "which circulated surreptitiously behind geographies." Like Blassingame, he yielded to a wanderlust. Instead of entering college at sixteen, he hoboed his way to the West Coast. Two years later, he went to college, and earned spending money by writing greeting verses. He settled in Texas with his family and began selling to the pulps.

In 1934, at the age of twenty-seven, he produced a blistering twenty-two-thousand-word extravaganza for DIME MYSTERY (March issue). His "Man Out of Hell" is an unusual blend of science fiction, mystery, menace and detection, topped off with a final, jolting, terrifying climax.

A cunning, inhuman creature is killing, burning away his victims' faces with quicklime. He can force his way up from under the ground, and walk under water with immunity. No matter what safeguards are taken, he successfully carries out the foreordained murders. The description of the monster patiently waiting a week in an air-tight glass case in the study of his next victim is a high point of suspense. Later, a report comes in of another murder. The killer has been forced into a swimming pool.

"With additional police reserves called, more than a hundred men surrounded the pool while it was drained. The slayer had disappeared into an eighteen-inch drain pipe. Hurrying to the other end of the drain, where it emptied into

the lake, officers with flashlights sighted the monster retreating into a bend of the huge pipe. Poison gas was pumped
into the pipe for thirty minutes. At the end of that time,
Detective Chris Lineman, protected by a gas mask, entered
the pipe's mouth. Seeing that the fiend was apparently unharmed and approaching, he retreated. In another moment,
the naked demon had come out of the pipe, and spraying the
stunning death rays, fought his way through a cordon of
police and plunged into the lake. The monster was not seen
after vanishing into the lake. Tracks found later on the
marshy shore, and two abandoned flat irons, indicated that
the demon had walked across the floor of the lake."

The menace is later revealed as a robot created out of
flesh-like rubber over a duralumin body. Radio-receiving
circuits control it. There is a television scanner in the head.
Tracking down the robot, Private Eye Bill Zeigler ends up
trapped in a vault-like room. He hides in a metal coffin.
"Through one of the holes he stared out into the room.
Wolff and the Hindu were moving toward the door. 'And
now,' said the doctor pleasantly, 'we'll fire the furnace.' "
This situation, with the hero waiting in an agony of anguished
anticipation as the coffins are thrust one by one into the
oven, is the very quintessence of fear-fiction thrills.

To be successful, a pulp writer had to produce a variety of
fiction: mysteries, westerns, detectives and the like. In
Knox' case, versatility took on a new meaning. For within
the confines of the weird menace formula, he remained to an
extent unclassifiable, while others often fell into the rut of
repeating themselves. His work ranged from the heart-
touching diary of a little girl to a grim psychological study of
an hallucinatory aberration, with many gradations in
between.

He was nothing if not modern, as seen in his "TV robot."

And generally, his story constructions were sound, as in "Nightmare" in DIME MYSTERY (May, 1934), which also has the air of freshness to it. A mysterious doctor and his patient, an invalid, are found murdered under strange circumstances. The investigation turns up the invalid's journal, and what emerges is an appalling account of a systematic weakening of the patient's will by the doctor. (He stands to profit by inheriting an estate.) Ostensibly, the idea was to explore the hidden world of the sleeping psyche. But in doing so, a monstrous, evil entity is released. Seemingly, this fright-figure has no real substance, existing only as a self-hypnotically induced aberration. The investigators piece together what happened.

" 'Then damn it, man, what killed them?'

" 'The beast,' said Fisher. 'The nightmare beast, the same beast that lurks deep in the subconscious of each of us . . . It was the human instinct in Vard's subconscious mind that perceived the truth of what was taking place. In trying to translate it to the conscious mind by using the symbol of the ape, it was doing what the subconscious mind always does in dreams. Every psychologist knows that. In this case the ape-symbol was so vivid, so real that it amounted to a genuine hallucination. When Vard, in his trance, felt the urgings of the beast, it seemed to him that it was an actual beast he followed, struggled against, succumbed to!' "

The four authors covered here, then, could be counted on for regularity and readability (not necessarily at the same time, as we have seen). A fifth name can be brought into the proceedings, to point up another aspect of the pulp writing game--the effect on the author, himself, rather than the reader. It's our friend, Norvell W. Page. His is an interesting case; I might say he is an example of split personality.

A native of Richmond, Virginia, Page worked for various

newspapers from 1924 until 1934, including the NEW YORK HERALD TRIBUNE, the NEW YORK TIMES and the NEW YORK WORLD-TELEGRAM. According to Mort Weisinger, he first appeared in print as a fiction writer under the name N. Wooten Poge, in DETECTIVE DRAGNET.

Working in the longer lengths suited Page. The same month his "Dance of the Skeletons" appeared, the first issue of THE SPIDER MAGAZINE hit the stands. R. T. Maitland Scott wrote the first two adventures. Then that December, Page took over, using the Grant Stockbridge house name, and during the next ten years, produced one hundred and sixteen Spider novels, while spewing out other pulp fiction of all kinds.

The author took to the character as readily as his readers-- it was one of the most popular pulp heroes. Later, Hollywood, made two Spider serials. Steeger tells how Page would "show up at the office with a black cape and dark slouch hat, wearing a Spider ring and stalking about as though he were going to perform some miracle of fiction."

Page reminded you somewhat of a bearded Mischa Auer. He was one of many writers who found the gentle climate of Florida conducive to creative thought. Anna Maria, not far from Tampa, became the stomping ground for The Spider and some of his fellow pulpsters. Blassingame, a font of anecdotal material on the period, recalls how he himself dreamed up his stories while walking along the beach. Another wrestled with his plots while sitting on the beach, with his children climbing over him. A third walked in the sand with his wife, exchanging ideas. And Page stormed about in hat and cape, muttering and gesturing, an eccentric figure indeed. "Since at that time there probably weren't more than one hundred persons in Anna Maria, it made a weird-looking sight: people talking to themselves and waving their hands on an otherwise deserted beach."

In his stories, Page showed a technical brilliance, plotting at a furious pace. His works displayed an innate sense of structure and dramatic flair. He blew up a wild storm of excitement. His plot-complication holes were filled like nature tackling a vacuum. The only trouble was, in all this frenzied free-wheeling, he sometimes forgot, or just didn't think it mattered, to tie up all the loose ends, a common failing among pulp practitioners.

During the war, Page became a specialist in writing government reports; later, he worked for the Atomic Energy Commission. In 1961, at the age of fifty-seven, he died of a heart attack.

When you consider the adaptations these and other writers made, it's possible to find a pattern in all this. Presentations became somewhat stereotyped, as they were worked over again and again. Look at them, and you'll find they can be divided into groups. Here are the main recurring themes; they fall under eight main headings.

1. **Compulsion-Obsession**: Here, the hero or heroine is brought to some act irresistably against his will or wishes. In "The Man Who Lost His Soul," by Norvell Page, in HORROR STORIES (October, 1935), a young man is resuscitated two hours after a leaking gas jet had stopped his pulse. The doctor who performs the revivification puts the idea in his head that while dead he had become a fiend from Hell. He is convinced he has no soul, and goes to the home of his fiancee to murder her. Her love saves him. They learn that the doctor, who had been infatuated with the heroine, had gained hypnotic control over him while his mind was impaired.

2. **Resurrection**: The general procedure was to have certain principals, such as the hero or heroine, seemingly arise from the dead. Usually, the explanation is that they weren't dead

after all. Sometimes, someone else is substituted for the person, as in Frances Bragg Middleton's "The Corpse Came Back," in DIME MYSTERY (June, 1934). An old grandfather who died returns to his family home, "a broken, terrified, quaking ruin of a man." He is later discovered to be the man's blacksheep cousin, who is involved in kidnapping and blackmail, and picked on the old established family home as a hideout, and in a typical flamboyant plot complication, assumed the corpse's identity as a disguise.

3. **Age vs. Youth**: Whenever the plot called for wheezy ancients, you knew that before long, shrinking young maidens would fall into their clutches. Senility was confoundingly paired with lechery. Sometimes, these oldsters could barely totter, but the vision of fair young flesh set them to frothing. Back then, there was a generation gap too, or should I say, degeneration gap? In "They Dare Not Die," in TERROR TALES (January, 1935), Nat Schachner tells of a couple touring the back stretches of the Adirondacks, who come upon a hidden retreat operated by a once-famous surgeon. He pretends to restore youth to his millionaire clients, who are nearing death, by extracting a fluid from the pituitary gland of a young person. The young couple arouse the lust of the old women and senile men, who hold an auction to bid on them.

4. **Weird Monsters**: The Hairless Thing and his companions appear from time to time. Francis James introduces several of his own in "Nursery of Horror," in HORROR STORIES (March, 1935). One has a "great, round, tallow-white head, with hideous, long mouth curved in an obscene oval with yellow fangs edging all around," and a bloated face with a single eye in the forehead. Another has two heads. The Human Crab is "a figure with the torso and head of a man but with seven legs attached around the body." They are the

Walter Baumhofer is back, with another of his beauties-to-be-buried-alive, for **Dime Mystery's** January, 1935 issue, illustrating James Duncan's "Food for Coffins." The cover later would appear on the April, 1940 **Dime Mystery**, when the magazine went through a reprint-cover phase, minus the NRA sign, of course, and with such edifying changes as nude gals in the caskets instead of men, and rents and tears in the heroine's clothes, at strategic points.

products of a doctor's experiments. He mates young women with freaks, then treats the expectant mothers with rays to hasten the development of the offspring and create monsters with scrambled genes.

5. Evil Crones: Next to masked villains and deformed creatures, the most utilized fear-figure was the gnarled old woman, hurling curses and maledictions on everyone. Such an old harridan, and her son, have a young couple at their mercy in Saul W. Paul's "Forest of Fear," in THRILLING MYSTERY (December, 1935). The hulking son, a doctor, has become weak-minded. His mother cackles: "You need a woman's brain, because it was a woman who made you lose the balance of your own. . .We'll have her brain out soon, Eben, cooking over the fire in its own blood. . ." Before they can sit down to dinner, the hero saves the day by shooting the son, and the old crone kills herself.

6. Curses and Spells: These were popular aggravation devices employed by the villain to scare everyone as he went about his nefarious activities. Usually, the curse was simply a bit of misdirection, as in "Blood Feast," in DIME MYSTERY (March, 1935). In this H. M. Appel story, the curse of the storm god is blamed for the deaths of the hero's ancestors, who all died on Devil Island. Apparently, the storm devil is behind the butcheries of members of the present family. However, the murderer is the architect who built the house--and various secret passageways--bent on torturing everyone with fear before killing them in insane jealousy.

7. Supernaturalism: This and the next classification are treated more fully later. Now and then an author strayed from the straight path of mystification logically explained, to explore the twists and turns of illusionary events. "The House of Doomed Brides," by Ray Cummings, in TERROR TALES (February, 1935), is one of the few fantasies this master of early science fiction wrote. This time, the curse is real. A young man in love with a girl is invited by her grandfather to visit their home, an old castle. The old man explains. "This family into which you would like to marry has a history--a tragic one. The present, young Earle, is but the past in the making. The future, too, will advance to the present, and fade away into the past." The legend handed down is that one of the wives, in times past, cast off her husband. He was a necromancer, and he cursed her and her issue, down through the ages. Each mother dies as her daughter is born. The grandfather has devised a mechanism to let him see the future, geared to operate in synchronization with the union of the three minds. They watch ten years go by, as the young man and girl marry, and have a child. Then the wife dies, as did her ancestors. Suddenly, there's a rumble, and the castle begins crumbling. They are found the next morning, the grandfather dead, and the couple aged ten years. The curse dies with the castle.

8. **Evil Temptress**: When an alluring, irresistible female comes on the scene, she is always bent on some deadliness that has to do with ensnaring the hero. He barely extricates himself in time to become reconciled to his fiancee or wife. "Caia the Cruel," by Paul Ernst, in DIME MYSTERY (July, 1935), is a story within a story. The hero, an architect, meets again the femme fatale, who has the manner of "one who could do anything--and who would do anything--her deep, passionate nature desired." She wants him to design a new home for her. Earlier, he had spurned her advances to him, to marry someone else. She is burning for revenge, while her equally lustful brother desires to subjugate the hero's wife. The young couple uncover a stone disc, brought back earlier from Africa. It is a Persian talisman, which can be "read." In it they see themselves in Rome, as slaves of Caia and her half-brother, embodiments of the revenge-minded seductress and her brother. When the strange vision ends, the couple decide to forgo a visit to the woman, who had been expecting them. A seething inferno of hate, she is left waiting impatiently to subject them to tortures in the slave cellar under her home.

CHAPTER V. PURPLE PROSE PROS

The pulpwoods are a vast jungle where, in-stead of giant orchids and remarkable butter-flies, the explorer finds only the familiar flora and fauna of more temperate climes, usually stunted in growth, tasteless to the palate, and proliferating with the speed of amoeba climax.

Fletcher Pratt
SATURDAY REVIEW OF LITERATURE
(July 3, 1937)

Now for a brief negative report. In the period surveyed so far, we've seen the authors adopting an extravagant style that sometimes bordered on the ludicrous. That is, at its worst. Soon, though, they began phasing it out in favor of a leaner, racier presentation. We can speculate that their excesses finally caught up to them. For during the so-called Gothic period, if there was anything more wretched than the grisly creatures portrayed so graphically, it was the slovenly writing habits repeated so frequently. The exigencies of the profession, of course, encouraged such transgressions. Slipshod work habits may have reached a record low with one mystery-a-day author, if the following story can be believed. It seems he wrote at such breakneck speed, never checking back, that editors could tell when he stopped for lunch. He would forget who was whom, and reverse the roles of his hero and villain. In this vein, here are a few "horrible examples" from the weird menace field.

Loose-Enditis--the failure to explain all the complications. For instance, the point is made in a story several times that drugs (a favorite motivational factor) were not behind the deviationist behavior of the characters. At the conclusion, what happens? You guessed it. Drugs were the cause after all. Another time, a ravening beast on a killing rampage remains unscathed when the hero fires point blank at it, leading to the inescapable conclusion that it must be super-natural. But later, the hero handily dispatches it with a sword, to reveal it as a huge wolf. Its seeming invulnerability is never explained. In another story, victims are found head-less, with no trace of blood about. But the matter of where the blood--and the heads--went is never cleared up--by the author, that is.

Non Sequitors --"Something hellish had got hold of him. One side of his face seemed torn off by the roots, skin and flesh ripped down as one would shuck an ear of corn. 'Look out for him! Put on a tourniquet and stop that bleeding!' I yelled back to the others." (Ye gods, where, around his neck?)

Anachronisms--"blind blackness," "striken charms," "lumi-nous black," "dreadful doom," "crafty cunning."

Cliches--One of the most persistent might be subtitled the Sore-Head Syndrome. The hero would be dashing here and there searching frantically for the heroine. Then, wham! He's slugged on the head. "Something hard and heavy descended sickenly against his skull, the words in his brain streamed into meaninglessness, and then there was nothing." Another: "Then a red-hot bomb burst in my head. . .and I knew no more." And a third: "And lightning flamed deep in his skull, a pinpoint of light that swelled and swelled until it encom-passed the universe in roaring oblivion." This was the most popular way to render the hero *hors de combat*, so that he could be neatly trussed up for the final scene in which the fiend threatens the heroine with all manner of nasty fates.

Such were some of the offenses committed by the pulps. Yet the thirty million or so readers each month didn't let these inelegancies bother them noticeably. They demanded fast-paced excitement, and they got it. To extend Hilaire Belloc's self-epitaph to the pulps: "Their sins were scarlet but their stories were read."

The August, 1936 **Ace-High Detective** (a Popular Publications pulp) continued the "nude" look in its first issue that detective magazines had been exploiting since the early thirties. Rafael M. de Soto is the artist here, with a scene from John Murray Reynolds' "The Creeping Doom," Li Ming's diabolic vengeance for having been sent to prison.

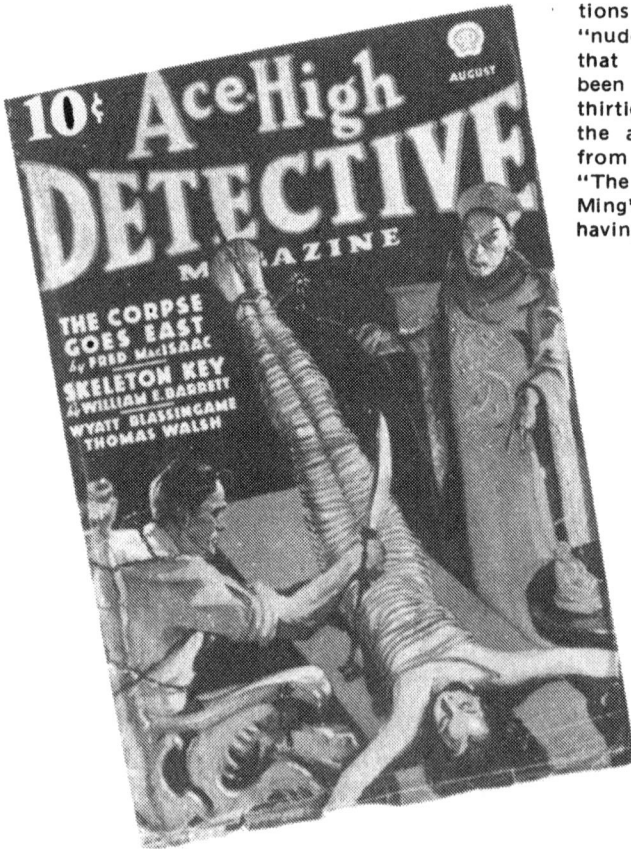

CHAPTER VI. FOUL FIENDS AND FAIR MAIDENS

If you get a title that catches on, then add a few more, you're in for a nice profit.

Martin Goodman

Pulp publishers were opportunists, if nothing else. They were quick to see the handwriting on the wall, or should I say, the printing on the page? As this burgeoning mystery format gained acceptance, competition increased. Several new pulp entries came out in 1935 and 1936, and continued to appear into the forties. Some did not have as much good, solid, hard-core weird menace as the Thrilling and Popular issues, but there was no doubt what they were trying to do.

MYSTERY ADVENTURES appeared March, 1935. For some reason known probably to no one today, the magazine went through several meaningless title changes. It became NEW MYSTERY ADVENTURES, then MYSTERY AD-VENTURE MAGAZINE, and finally reverted back to MYS-TERY ADVENTURES, when Harold Hersey, in another of his short-lived publishing ventures, took it over. Early issues sold at the odd pulp price of twenty cents, which was later dropped to fifteen cents, the same as HORROR STORIES and TERROR TALES, but of course, five cents more than most pulps, including THRILLING MYSTERY.

The company might have been called, The House of Hubbard. It seemed there were at least four or five Hubbards involved, when there probably weren't more than three, at the most. For several issues, the publisher was Pierre Publications, with A. R. Roberts as editor, and Stanley Hubbard, editor of SAUCY ROMANTIC ADVENTURES, as business manager. Walter W. Hubbard, credited as a colonel, wrote a column called "Broadway and Hollywood." From this it is apparent that the magazine made no effort to capture just one type of reader, as the variety of the contents proved. Actually, more attention seemed to be paid to retitling and personal name changes than to story promotion. By 1936, the company's name was Fiction Magazines, Inc. Now the Broadway column carried the byline, W. Whiteley Hubbard (the Colonel?). The Rev. W. W. Hubbard was listed as editor (the colonel-columnist?). By November of that year, H. D. Hubbard (another brother?) was editing the magazine, with Stanley Hubbard still as business manager. What was going on here? Were the Hubbard brothers (two? three?) just trying to get editorial mileage out of their name, or were they cursed with a lack of parental imagination in their names? The next issue, Harold Hersey took over, and continued the publication into 1937.

Hersey's is one of the failure stories of the pulps. The guy just never seemed to get a consistent line going for long. In 1919, he edited the first eight issues of THE THRILL BOOK, for Street & Smith. He later called this early fantasy-oriented effort a miserable fiasco, although in its sixteen issues appeared many fine stories, including Francis Stevens' celebrated five-part serial, "The Heads of Cerberus."

Then he went to W. M. Clayton as head editor, later becoming supervisory editor with Bernarr Macfadden's publications. He co-founded and edited the Original Hersey Magazines, which included FLYING ACES, THE DRAGNET, UNDERWORLD MAGAZINE, MURDER STORIES and others. Also, he published GANGSTER STORIES, RACKE-TEER STORIES, MOBS, DETECTIVE TRAILS, GHOST STORIES and MIRACLE SCIENCE FICTION AND FAN-TASY STORIES. Financially, he did well until the stock market collapse, which hit him hard.

At the time he bought MYSTERY ADVENTURES, he was trying to capitalize on the popularity of comic strip characters by placing them in pulp stories. It was a questionable plan, to say the least. He published one issue each of FLASH GORDON and DAN DUNN, and two of TAILSPIN TOMMY. It's ironic that some of the magazines put out by Hersey, that either bombed or fizzled at the time, generating few financial sparks, today are among the most expensive of collectors' items. FLASH GORDON STRANGE ADVEN-TURE MAGAZINE is not necessarily the rarest, but it fetches more than one hundred dollars. Issues of THE THRILL BOOK bring more than fifty dollars each.

Hersey came up with a publishing credo in the December issue of MYSTERY ADVENTURES that has a familiar ring. "I've put everything but the kitchen sink, and by this I mean, that you'll find included in the following pages the most thrilling selection of yarns that has come my way in a long, long while. . .I'll eat the page this is written on if this isn't the best fifteen cents worth of entertaining stories to be found anywhere for the price!" Pulp editors had strange appetites.

After his fling with this publication, he seemed to be catching his breath, or perhaps settling his stomach, until the forties. In 1941, he tried to make a go of it again, with such humor and joke magazines as KHAKI WEEKLY, YOO-HOO, ARMY LIFE. These, too, soon disappeared.

Getting back to MYSTERY ADVENTURES: each issue

The October, 1936 **Mystery Adventure Magazine** shows Saunders to advantage, as he shows Zenith Rand's space companion to advantage.

gave the reader a potpourri of story subjects--a space opera, for instance, a foreign legion adventure, a few weird menace offerings. Either the editor couldn't make up his mind what to emphasize, or else he felt the variety would give everybody something. In that respect, the publication resembled THE THRILL BOOK, which mixed adventure with fantasy and the weird. The pace was not as leisurely as in THE THRILL BOOK; the stories had more verve, even if they weren't necessarily better.

MYSTERY ADVENTURES gave sex a passing nod in the illustrations, but kept the story line straight and true. Several covers drew on the considerable talents of Norman Saunders, with his lush, voluptuous females, a few wisps of clothing barely covering their charms. Some of the interior drawings showed near nudes, although it was obvious from reading the stories that this was a case of artistic license.

Weird menace authors appearing here were Wayne Rogers, Richard Race Wallace, Hugh B. Cave, Nat Schachner and Richard Tooker. Some of the talents were notable, such as Octavus Roy Cohen and Frank Bunce, who also sold to the slicks.

The "Age vs Youth" theme appears in Rogers' "Tomorrow They Die," which echoes Schachner's earlier TERROR TALES story, "They Dare Not Die," even to a similarity of title. Here the villain lures young women to a private lodge where a group of senile, tubercular men live under his charge. Knowing they are nearing death, they willingly pay large sums for the women at beauty auctions. Weird menace trappings include floggings and a black mass. Later, the old men's "brides" are placed alive in the caskets with their expired paramours, to be buried alive much as Egyptian wives were.

The stylization here was typical of much pulp fiction, where the maladjusteds, evildoers and just plain dirty old men were allowed to have all the fun (provided they got their comeuppance), while the hero's reward usually was nothing more than a chaste kiss.

The same year MYSTERY ADVENTURES started, a company with the deceptive name of Culture Publications was putting out the Spicy line, which included SPICY MYSTERY (not much mystery, but plenty of spice), under editor, Lawrence Cadman. Spicy covers were for the voyeuristic, mainly. The gals wore very little. They were menaced, if that's the word, by tough-looking thugs, sometimes, strange creatures hardly more frightening than Halloweeners. These scenes had a static, posed quality to them, even if they did cause avid eye movement.

If the customer didn't balk at the high price--twenty-five cents a copy--then probably he didn't mind the fact that there was less reading matter than in any other regular-sized pulp. Stories were short, not more than six thousand words or so, and profusely illustrated. The titillating drawings, rich in anatomical detail, contributed more to the magazine's sales than the stories themselves, which often were no more than suggestive sketches.

Every once in a while, though, something of more substance seemed to sneak in. This example from the third issue of SPICY MYSTERY (July, 1935) is a rare combination of typical Spicy licentiousness, and a trenchant murder involvement. In "Crimson Heart," by Ken Cooper, a physician finds himself fatally attracted to an exotic Russian exile. Over the protests of his wife, he goes to her home. The alluring woman is attended by a hideous deaf mute, who always seems to be hovering about.

The female of the species could be as deadly as the male, in these weird-menace imbroglios, as shown here in "Baal's Daughter," by Cornell Woolrich, **Thrilling Mystery,** January, 1936.

Later, the doctor is obsessed with a fantasy-exhilaration of her body against his. He succumbs to his aroused instincts and decides to kill the servant so he can possess her. Once more, he goes to her house. He peers through the window and sees the servant kneeling beside the woman, fondling her body. He goes to the front door, and when the servant answers, stabs him with a scalpel. It might be pointed out that unlike Popular and sometimes Thrilling, this line did not affect an oppressive and foreboding manner; Spicy stories were clear and concise, if usually shallow otherwise:

"It seemed natural that I should say something as I walked into her parlor. 'I have killed Boris,' I said.

"Her hand came to her white throat, tensed there. I fully expected her to scream, but her lips were silent. I dropped my bag and crossed the room, kneeling beside her.

" 'There was nothing else!' I panted. 'I saw him touching you with his hands . . . with his vile lips. It was sacrilege!. ' "

When he tries to make love to her, she stops him. " 'We must be free,' she whispered, 'free of everything.' " He understands. He goes home. His wife is in bed. He leaps toward her. "There was a muffled squoosh as the blade bit into her white throat; a hollow rattle deep down in her chest."

He buries the body under the floor boards. Then he hears a tell-tale muffled pounding, a thump, thump, thump. Finally, he pries up the boards and lifts out the dead body and cuts open the chest to rip out the heart. He takes it to lay at the woman's feet.

When he arrives, he finds her dead, a knife in her heart. He is committed to an asylum. Outside his cell, he hears voices discussing his case. One refers to the woman and her servant. " 'They were husband and wife . . . Married in Russia before the war.' " And a moment later, the other voice comments that the wife's body was found under the floor, when someone heard the ticking of her wrist watch.

It may be that this example glitters because of the sur-
rounding dross. But there is a dramatic quality to it, that sets
it apart, and considerable skill in the double twist. While
salaciousness was limited to the appropriate circumstances
in this story, lasciviousness ran rampant elsewhere. Here are
a few typical descriptions.

- Her body was sheer perfection; an impossible dream come to life. He touched
her breasts, caressed her narrow, feminine hips with his palms. His head sank;
his lips glued to the hollow of her throat,
wandered toward the silk-smooth area
between her breasts. . .

- Her large, firm breasts were like mounds
of snow under the powerful light. They
rose and fell spasmodically, trembling
with agitation.

- Smooth, shapely legs tapering to small
ankles. Full rounded thighs that swelled
out into curving hips. A slim waist. The
pulse-quickening glory of her bosom. . .

A line comes to mind from Mae West's "Diamond Lil:"
"What are you doing, making love or taking inventory?" It
seems that the Spicy authors were always taking inventory,
no matter whether anyone was making love or not. Every
woman on the scene was always a ravishing creature–
whether maid, matron or mother. And all her assets had to
be catalogued before the action could start again. This could
lead to such absurdities as in a later story where the hero
spies a damsel some hundred feet away, at night, and notes
the shape of her breasts, the turn of her ankles, even the
color of her eyes.

Such compulsive erotica would hardly bring a blush to the youngest reader today. Then, it was pretty hot stuff. And those three-dot pauses every now and then when the hero and heroine fell into a compromising situation. Ah! There was no doubt about what that meant. A funny thing, though. For all their sexual blatancy, the magazines (including ADVENTURE, DETECTIVE, WESTERN, preceded by the word, SPICY) missed a bet. Story titles weren't suggestive at all, except in a few cases. They went along these lines: "Hands of the Dead," "Death at High Noon," "Corpse Without a Face," "Fangs of the Bat," "Madman's Menace," "Dark Splendor," "Fiends' Feast," "Mansion of Monsters," "Doom Door."

While the Spicy line was not held in high repute, nevertheless, it offered a quick sale for acceptable material. As one author notes, "If I needed money (and I generally did), I could take them a story in the morning, come back and get a check in the afternoon. They needed copy. So when I had a reject from the regular pulps, I could rewrite, remove the young boy who helped the hero, replace him with a seventeen-year-old girl with no clothes on, and usually get paid."

Rafael M. de Soto also had an **Ace Mystery** cover to his credit, the September, 1936 issue, a short-lived publication that presented as good a selection as any horror-terror pulp of its kind.

Another Saunders cover, for the November, 1936 issue, finds the Domino Lady peculiarly unaware of her look-alike nemesis. Saunders' women were among the more ravishing seen on covers.

Both MYSTERY ADVENTURES and SPICY MYSTERY can be called peripheral menace pulps. ACE MYSTERY, which came out in 1936 and ran but three issues, was a full-fledged mystery-terror entry. (By now, it's obvious what one word was the most popular title in a publisher's lexicon.) A. A. Wyn's Magazine Publishers conceived of the new publication as a competitor to such established pulse-quickeners as HORROR STORIES, TERROR TALES, DIME MYSTERY and THRILLING MYSTERY. Publisher of record for ACE MYSTERY was Periodical House. This was a subsidiary of the parent company, headed by Wyn's wife, Rose. Mainly, Wyn took care of the men's pulps--westerns, detectives, aviation--and his wife handled the love pulps and later, confession magazines. She was also listed as editor of SECRET AGENT X. The company used the "Ace" designation for its imprint. Harry Widmer served as editor on many of the titles in the thirties; he went with Popular in the forties.

Wyn started out as a writer, after the usual odd jobs. He had been a cowboy in Wyoming, a merchant seaman and schoolteacher in Idaho. He began editing pulps for Dell in 1926, where Steeger got his start, too. His name was Aaron Weinstein, but early in his writing career, he changed it because he believed in numerology, and the letters of his new name added up to one, the best number. The second "A" never did have a name attached to it (like Arthur Burks' middle initial, J). Donald Wollheim, a long-time Wyn editor (who today publishes the DAW line of paperbacks) notes that Wyn was a confirmed atheist who made a special practice of going to work on all religious holidays, and even frowned on closing for Christmas. "But after the death of his son, he made a complete reversal and became very religious. When he was dying, the last thing he did was have his nurse read to him from the Bible (which by then he almost knew by heart, for he could and did quote from it at editorial meetings)." Wyn died in 1967 of cancer, at the age of sixty-nine.

He made an unusual contribution to the pulps, above and beyond the call of duty, that he never received full credit for. During the thirties, the pulps often drew condemnation from many quarters. They were castigated as a menace to young readers, as a graveyard for creative talent, and as a sop to the reading tastes of the lowest common denominator. As soon as a blast was leveled at the pulp bulwarks, there was Wyn rushing to the breech. Other publishers rarely bothered to defend their business, much less take on the role of public protector.

When a NEW YORK TIMES editor referred to the pulps as a "little known and certainly officially unrecognized" business, in which "volume of production is more important than literary quality" (August 28, 1935), Wyn quickly responded. He cited facts and figures to show that far from being unrecognized, it catered to thirty million readers a month and paid writers one and a half million dollars a year. And again, when a pulp author took the profession to task in THE AMERICAN MERCURY (March, 1936), he snapped back with another spirited rebuttal. He may have spent as much time watchdogging papers and periodicals, as attending to his own business interests.

The Wyns bought Magazine Publishers from Harold Hersey, who had started it in 1928. Hersey had incorporated a symbol on the cover of THE DRAGNET MAGAZINE; this publication later became DETECTIVE DRAGNET. The representation was a blue swastika straight up and down (rather than slanted, as was the Nazi sign), on a white field in a red circle. It was an ancient good-luck signature--which didn't do much for Hersey, certainly. Wyn changed it to a black ace of spades after Hitler's accession to power. Cover symbols were popular with several publishers. Popular's covers carried the famous white PP initials, the first one reversed. They were printed over a blue, later purple, background, which itself was outlined by a curved white border. On the weird menace line, this seal was particularly appropriate, since viewed from a distance, it appeared to be a skull.

When Wyn issued ACE MYSTERY, the Gothic style was on the way out, with sex-sadism becoming more obvious.

According to Wollheim, Wyn's heart just wasn't in weird menace, although he featured it from time to time in 10 DETECTIVE ACES, the mid-thirties continuation of DE-TECTIVE DRAGNET. But even if he didn't try hard, the three issues of ACE MYSTERY contained as many good stories as any three issues you could select in this line, reflecting Wyn's maxim: "The story's the thing. . .Good writing never has spoiled a well-plotted pulp story, but it never made a bad one good."

Frederick C. Davis led off each of the three issues. He was another of the pulp speed demons. At the time, he was a million-word-a-year producer--actually, one and a quarter million words--with his mystery and detective pieces. These included series characters like Carter Cole, in DIME DE-TECTIVE, the Moon Man, in 10 DETECTIVE ACES, and the Ravenwood novelettes in SECRET AGENT X. In addition, he wrote the OPERATOR #5 novels which, he says "in time got to be too much in addition to my other work, and I had to beg off. I'm not sure, but I think Emile Tepperman took over. It's easy to tell our work apart, because I used footnotes and he didn't.

"Before the pulps began to fade, I turned to doing mystery books for The Crime Club. After thirty or so more I turned to Dodd, Mead for six, then back to Doubleday again for one more, published in 1971. Six of these were condensed in COSMOPOLITAN." His most recent book was called "Trap #6," written under the pen name of Stephen Ransome. So, we meet another author who made the transition from pulps to slicks effortlessly. Davis now lives in Florida.

He began writing for pulp magazines while attending Dartmouth in 1924. By the time ACE MYSTERY came on the scene, he was among the most successful pulp authors going. His three "terror novels" for Ace were presented from the viewpoint of the heroine, like Zagat's. Only his stories moved rapidly, with very little time out for reflection and self-appraisal. Using females as the protagonists may have been coincidence, he says now, "but more likely it was by choice, simply because women become terrified and horrified more easily than men."

His three novels can be summarized very briefly. In one, the heroine is brought to a murderous frenzy by a sustained, high-pitched note. This is finally discovered to originate at a directional reflector loudspeaker, aimed at the victim. (The author mistakenly visualizes sound as a directional wave, like light.) In another story, the heroine and hero investigate a sculptor who displays tiny figurines that turn out to be corpses shrunk to a diminuitive size. The third one concerns a series of murders of old people at a sanitarium, where a turbulent lake holds an eerie fascination for the heroine. In each, Davis' skill at plotting and developing dramatic intensity keeps the pace brisk and the reader anxious to find out what happens next.

Like Zagat, Blassingame and several others, Davis found that personal contacts played a large part in subsequent sales. He has this to say about it.

"Pulp writers and pulp editors operated under a simple system of availability. At the time when my work was most in demand, and the pulps were at their height, I was living smack in the middle of Manhattan, practically next door to the publishers' offices, except for Munsey, which was downtown, near the financial district.

"It was my practice to take an idea or two into an editor's office to get an okay before writing it, and I often talked shop with editors over lunch. Most writers lived in New York or nearby and kept in close touch with the editors, both through personal visits to their offices or over the phone.

"Editors often phoned me to ask for a story of a certain type and a certain length, and of course, I would immediately oblige. I grew to be close personal friends with Harry Widmer, Wyn's chief editor, and with Charles Ingerman, who was first an assistant editor with Munsey, then editor of DETECTIVE FICTION WEEKLY for a short while (no editor stayed put for very long with Munsey), and later an assistant at Popular Publications under Rogers Terrill, where he edited copy for OPERATOR #5. Another editor at Wyn's office, alongside Widmer, was Helen Wismer--strange, the similarity of those two names. Helen was a highly intelligent, very personable young woman who soon left her editorial chair to marry James Thurber.

"Essentially, what I'm saying here is that the pulp field was no different than other fields of publishing, in that personal and professional relationships between writers and editors often overlapped."

Other authors in ACE MYSTERY were John Knox, one of the busiest of the horror-terror writers, Hugh B. Cave, G. T. Fleming-Roberts, who was practically a homesteader in THRILLING MYSTERY, Henry Treat Sperry, Paul Ernst, and Paul Chadwick, who wrote the SECRET AGENT X novels under the Brant House byline.

Now, this business of weird menacism--fiends with evil designs on fair young maidens, if you will--was certainly not confined so far just to the publications already mentioned. You could find many examples elsewhere. For our purposes, we're concentrating on the short-story publications, as contrasted to the series-character type, that emphasized this particular origination. Here are a few other sources. Some of the super-hero--or super-villain--adventures contained weird elements. THE SPIDER often faced situations that at first defied a logical explanation, and strongly suggested a supernatural cause. . .G-8 AND HIS BATTLE ACES regularly came up against uncanny and even impossible happenings. DOCTOR DEATH, a Dell publication, the occult scientist bent on mastering the world, qualifies as a "weird menace," but of course, is a book-length series character. The short stories were similar to those in HORROR STORIES, TERROR TALES or THRILLING MYSTERY. In one, a scientist changes into a kill-maddened ape. In another, the victims are done in by a black orchid that sprouts out of the pores on their faces. THE OCTOPUS and THE SCORPION (both written by Norvell Page), contained some weird menace stories, as did STAR DETECTIVE, SUPER DETECTIVE and Thrilling's BLACK BOOK DETECTIVE.

Hugh Cave for one helped keep many of these publications going as, for instance, the August, 1935 issue of STAR DETECTIVE, which contains his thirty-thousand word "Death Stalks the Night," a combination of weird menace and super hero pulp formulas, and the SUPER DETECTIVE line, which also featured Robert E. Howard. There were several pulps along these lines--MYSTERY ADVENTURES was one--that, because of the diversity of story presentations, never quite caught on with the reading public. They could still come up now and then with some top-notch efforts, though. It's just that finding examples from them today is more a matter of luck than perseverance, since many of these non-classifiables not only didn't catch on with the readers when they came out, but have been largely ignored by fans and collectors today.

CHAPTER VII. "THE SPEED MERCHANT OF THE PULPS"

Editors would call me up and ask me to do a novelette by the next afternoon and I would, but it nearly killed me. . .I once appeared on the covers of eleven magazines the same month, and then almost killed myself for years trying to make it twelve. I never did.

Arthur J. Burks

If overwork kills an author, then Arthur J. Burks, now in his seventies, must be a medical wonder. He's still alive and well, travels on lectures so frequently that his wife doesn't see him for weeks at a time, and occasionally dashes off an article. . .long after he set a killing pace as a million-word-a-year pulp producer in the thirties.

In fact, most years during that decade, he came closer to two million words published, and wrote much more than that, even, that he discarded or that editors rejected. His output covered the field: adventure, mystery, science fiction, detective, even love stories, under the name, Esther Critchfield. In the mystery-terror vein alone, he averaged about two stories a month for more than ten years. He aimed at an unbelievable eighteen thousand words a day, which must have made him the closest thing to perpetual motion we know.

Burks was of the "Look, Ma, no hands" school. He was a natural storyteller, who could write anytime, and get his ideas from everywhere. Once he sat down at his typewriter, he usually didn't get up until he had finished. He was a born word juggler, who could throw sentences into the air and have them land in place every time. He never had to revise . . .or at least, never did. To keep on schedule, he didn't have time to rewrite, and at two to three cents a word, which was what he was getting, he felt he couldn't afford to. Also, it was a matter of temperament. Once he completed a story, he couldn't rewrite it; he lost all creative affinity with it. When an editor once asked him to change one of his stories, Burks tried and finally, just discarded it. So he didn't make that mistake again, he says.

A fellow writer of the time noted: "Burks can sit down at the typewriter without an idea in his head and pick any object in his New York hotel room–a lamp shade, for example. Within a page of writing, it has taken on the sinister implications of a certain mandarin's headgear, starting Burks along an Oriental trail that has netted him eight million words on a single typewriter he owned. If he doesn't make four hundred dollars a week, he feels he's going stale."

He made more than that some weeks. But it's been reported that over the years, he often averaged less.

Along this same line, G. T. Fleming-Roberts remarked how Burks once built a story around a glass doorknob, which concealed a diamond. After that, he said, "the entire detective field became cluttered with stories concerning stolen diamonds concealed in anything of cut glass from Lady Windfall's punchbowl to milady's perfume bottle stoppers."

SIX DOORS
To HORROR

By Arthur J. Burks

This was one of Burks' more orthodox ghost stories, in **Terror Tales,** March, 1935. The artist is Amos Sewell, illustrating "Six Doors to Horror."

Early in his writing career, Burks earned the title, "Speed Merchant of the Pulps," a rank only slightly below the "King of the Pulps," the title held by Max Brand (whose real name was Frederick Faust). Along with Max Brand and H. Bedford-Jones, who jumped from one typewriter to another to keep three stories going at the same time, he ranked as one of the busiest one-man production lines of the times.

Just as the pulp magazine is the twentieth century lineal descendent of the nineteenth century dime novel, so Burks and his fellow super producers were the modern manifestation of earlier novel-a-week word merchants like Ned Buntline, Edward L. Wheeler and Colonel Prentiss Ingraham.

Buntline, whose real name was Edward Zane Carroll Judson, made Buffalo Bill famous with a series of "true-life" frontier sagas for Street & Smith's NEW YORK WEEKLY in the eighteen sixties and seventies. He boasted that he "never blotted out anything I have once written and never made a correction or modification." Yep, that's what he said. Wheeler wrote the Deadwood Dick novels for Beadle and Adams. One time they needed a serial in a hurry, so Beadle--the "inventor" of the dime novel--locked Wheeler in a room with a stack of paper. Two days later, he had his thirty-thousand-word cliff-hanger. Ingraham once dashed off a thirty-three-thousand word story in twenty-four hours. . .and in longhand, don't forget.

There's no report that an anxious publisher ever locked Burks into a room. He wouldn't have had to, since Burks was one of the strongest self-motivators going. He dashed off an eighty-thousand-word novel in ten days himself. Like Brand, he might end up as practically the only author in a specific issue of a pulp. One month he had five stories at one time in THRILLING ADVENTURES, one under his own name, and four under house names. Yes, other speed demons could top this. Walter B. Gibson, who wrote two Shadow novels a month, is a familiar example. Lester Dent, author of Doc Savage, under the Kenneth Robeson house name, is reputed to have produced fifty-six thousand words as a day's work, thirty-two thousand by dictaphone and twenty-four thousand by typewriter. But here we're talking mainly about a pre-sold series about a stock character, in novel-length format. The amazing thing about Burks' output was that most was in the short story and novelette form.

He may have been the most compulsive writer ever. This is how he described himself (WRITER'S DIGEST, June, 1937):

"When I'm not writing or thinking about a story, there's no living with me. I pace the floor. My family gets out of my way or gets stepped on. My children get kicked across the room. . .If the telephone rings, I bite the ear off the caller when I say hello. . .I hear every sound and it rasps on my nerves like a rusty file drawn over a rusty rasp. Absence of sound is even more maddening. I hate my food and drink. I hate everybody, including myself. I can't stay inside. I won't go out."

That was the author in his high-pressure prime. But when he started his writing career, while a young lieutenant in the Marines in 1920, his production pace was misleadingly slow, and his income ridiculously low. That year he made $3.58 in fiction sales, he recalls. "The second year I began writing prolifically; I set out to write two thousand words a day. I wrote in longhand, then typed it. The second year I made $1.57." Then his income started to pick up. By the fifth year, he was earning five hundred dollars. He left the service in 1928 to write full-time. Within two years, he was putting out a hundred thousand words a month, and bringing in better than two hundred weekly, in the midst of the Depression.

Rudolph Belarski's May, 1937 cover is for "Devil's Ransom" by George Wilson (one of the house names Margulies used for these short-shorts written to back up the cover). Scenes similar to this were appearing at this time on other publications, the main difference being, that elsewhere, the victims had little or no clothes on; while Thrilling kept the feminine charms fairly well covered up.

He didn't sell everything he wrote; it just seemed that way. Even his rejects found a home. He sent a story to Clayton Publications in 1930. This company published a string of pulps, such as ACE-HIGH, RANCH ROMANCES, JUNGLE STORIES, CLUES, ASTOUNDING STORIES and STRANGE TALES. A Clayton editor turned down Burks' submission and sent it back to Los Angeles, where the author had been living. But he had moved in the meantime, without leaving a forwarding address. So the manuscript found its way back to Clayton. The same editor bought it, thinking that the changes he had requested had been made, and the story was printed.

Since Burks refused to revise anything, his rejects kept piling up in boxes on the floor. With the Depression, several authors having trouble making sales, took to calling on Burks, who was basking in regular sales each month. They asked if they could take some of his rejected pieces and send them in under their own names. "Sure," Burks said, "as long as you let the editors know what you're doing." With a little doctoring, most of these yarns sold the second time around.

There are two surprising aspects to Burks' productivity. One has already been mentioned. He rarely wrote novels and serials, the ideal way to inflate your word count. And too, he wasn't an idea man; he got by largely on mood pieces, one of the most difficult structures to perfect. Come to think of it, though, that's probably why he could put out so prodigiously (provided he was so temperamentally constituted): he didn't have to devise plots with a lot of complications.

So what else did Burks do besides write, eat, sleep, and cash his checks? Well, he actually found time for a few other activities. It's a matter of record. He was quite active in the American Fiction Guild, which he helped organize and he served as its president for four years. The guild met for Friday luncheons, and just about all the pulp editors and writers in New York City popped in sooner or later. Steve Fisher recalls a get-together he attended (WRITER'S 1941 YEAR BOOK):

"Here was bearded Norvell Page. . .Opposite him sat Lester Dent. . .Down the line sat George Bruce, probably the best writer in the pulps. . .Paul Ernst was present, and Robert J. Hogan, author of the book-length magazines WU FANG and G-8--at one hundred and twenty thousand words a month! He had come with Edythe Seims, young and very pretty, who was editor of these two publications.

"Harry Widmer dropped in with Arch Whitehouse and Joe Archibald. Somewhere in the crowd sat Emile C. Tepperman, Richard Sale, Arthur Leo Zagat. . .

"But in the middle of the luncheon there was a sudden silence. Fifty people stopped eating and looked up. Leo Margulies made his usual dramatic entrance. Behind him came the stalwarts of his staff: George Post. . .Charles Ingerman. . .Mortimer Weisinger. . .I thought for a moment President Art Burks was going to leap to his feet and salute. I wouldn't have been surprised if he'd done this, and had said: 'The Fiction Guild is present and accounted for, sir . . . We have two new members, a Steve Fisher and a Frank Gruber. They have been vouched for by Lieutenant Ed Bodin, but I myself am not sure they can stay--since they have not met the requirements of this club: that of having five stories published in national magazines.'

"But Art kept his seat, and Leo Margulies and staff melted into the gathering. It was all very fine; except when I leaned over to ask Leo about a short-short I had submitted. Art cut in and said: 'See here, young man, we do not discuss shop at this luncheon.' "

As for Burks' fiction--the quality of his mood pieces varied. At their best, they caught the reader in an ocean swell of anticipation and beached him breathless and limp. They had an ingenuous manner that made the characters seem very human. They always "felt right," a fact that speeded sales. This is evident in the unconnected "On the Spot" series he wrote for Popular Publications in 1936. Here is the eclectic talent that allowed him to pick a subject, any subject, and dash off several thousand salable words on it.

He even turned his skills to promotional advantage. A notarized statement accompanied each story, stating that the author had drawn his inspiration from visiting the particular locale used in the story, such as the death house at Ossining, New York, a morgue, and a cemetery, and had conceived the story "on the spot." Two witnesses added substance to his claim: Ed Bodin, his friend and a literary agent, and L. Ron Hubbard, an adventure story super producer, later to become a top-flight science fiction author, and finally, the force behind dianetics and scientology.

Then followed a brooding study, strong on atmospherics. In each, the author evokes a feeling of imminent doom. There is little plot. In fact, "The Chair Where Terror Sat," in HORROR STORIES (June-July, 1936), is stream of consciousness, pure and simple. But what an effect. It describes the feelings of the author himself, as the executioner straps him in the electric chair.

"The straps were pulled tightly, but they didn't cover my mouth. The wet sponges dripped cold water on my leg and on my skull. At the panel the executioner stood, grinning, eager.

"I could see the white ghosts sleeping, in the black room beyond. One of them was a table I would soon be lying on,

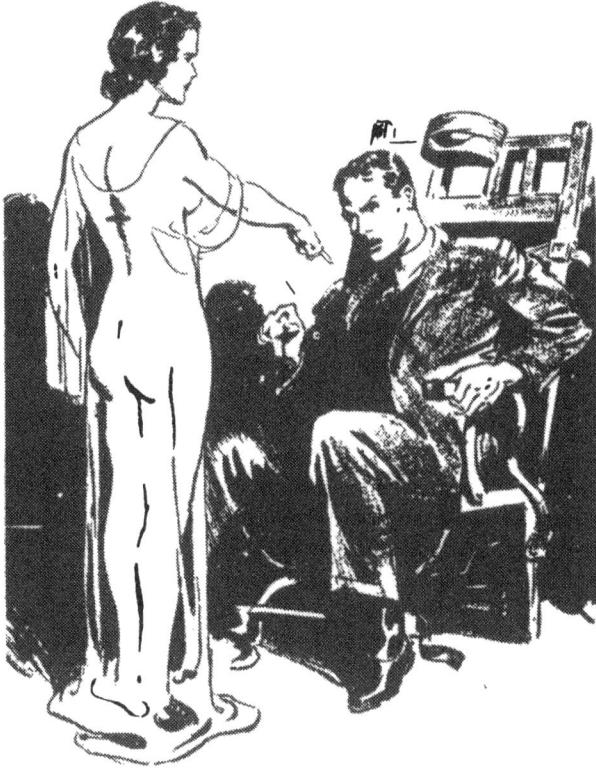

Steam-of-consciousness characterizes this Burks story, "The Chair Where Terror Sat," with its notarized attachment that the author created it "on the spot" during a visit to the Ossining prison, when he tried out the "hot seat."

only I wouldn't know it . . .

"Something hit me all over. The blow was so hard I didn't even feel it, though it drove me through the straps as if I had been hurled from a catapult . . .

"I was spirit now, it seemed, free from pain, while there in the grisly chair was all that remained of what I had been. . .

"I came to life, among the living, to find that it was dawn. I was stiff and sore. My friends said, as I was unfastened, that my hair was greying. I didn't speak, I merely gestured feebly . . ."

It seems that Burks could go on and on in this manner indefinitely. You might almost call him a modern-day Dante at times, able to take the reader with him into the innermost depths of his own psyche--providing a strangely personal experience unlike that offered by any other pulp author. During his "atmospheric period" (1935-1937), his work reveals a high quota of atypical themes, in which the conflict within is the dominant strain. The hero or heroine strives to overcome enigmatic threats which turn out later to be either figments of the imagination, or in some strange way, dangers perceived by them alone. Here are three instances.

1. The hero tries to save a Chinese girl he loves from the vengeance of the tong. She had mysteriously disappeared while they were in an elevator together. He is captured by masked Chinese and is to be killed with her. After losing consciousness, he awakens back in the elevator, alone. He searches the building, but finds no trace of the girl or the rooms where the weird events took place, or even any indication that anything had happened.

2. An old doctor, who knows he is dying, must steel himself to operate on his granddaughter, who has a serious internal disorder. The spirit of his enemy, who had earlier died, returns to haunt him and try to prevent the operation.

3. A picnic excursion becomes a frenzied search for a way out of a forest. The hero and heroine try to go back the way they came, but find themselves enclosed by the trees. Not a sound is heard. All woodland creatures have fled. As they proceed, they come upon first one, then another, of their friends. One has been crucified to a tree; two others have been buried. Their unexplainable deaths involve him in some ambiguous way. The stigmata appears on his hands, and other wounds on other parts of his body. The pair at length find the way past the wall, where they first entered. Their friends

are waiting for them, unharmed, after all.

Through much of Burks' material runs a mystical note, more evident than usual in this story.

"I never told anyone of the reddish discolorations on the soles of my feet, nor of the bleeding gash in my side. The gash, of course, might have been caused by a branch striking me in the dark. But how explain the marks on my feet? Except by this: I was a doubter--Had an All Wise Providence thus, by a seeming miracle, sought to show me the error of my ways of thought?"

A stark, bitter strain runs through "Devils in the Dust," in THRILLING MYSTERY (December, 1935), one of the grimmest, most pitiless horror accounts you'll find in the pulps, atmospherically, as bleak as a Siberian winter. Summarizing it can't convey the effect, but it will show the approach used. A man takes his bride to his home. They are almost trapped there by a pack of snarling dogs, avid for the remains of his parents, who had been buried behind the cabin. They escape as a dust storm whips up. Soon, it is a blinding frenzy.

"Through the cataclysmic devils' drone of the storm came other clamorous sounds. More dogs, everywhere. . .I heard, often, the shrill, birdlike cries of the women. . .It was always the young girls who screamed through the storm."

They come upon a girl, fending off a madman. The hero kills him, and recognizes in the assailant the lay-preacher who had married them earlier that day. They go on, unable to see, barely able to breathe. They find another struggling pair, and again, the hero overcomes him. The second man is the same preacher.

The storm gets worse. He has to carry his wife, in a sling on his back. Suddenly, she's snatched away. He searches through the stinging dust, and finds her in the clutches of three men. These men, too, are the same as the preacher. He succeeds in freeing her, and they barely creep ahead.

"With each cough more dirt sucked into my lungs. Norma was coughing too. I turned her against me, put my lips against her lips. . .it was like kissing the dry dirt on which we lay, panting."

At length, they find themselves among other people. The group comes out of the storm. Leading them is the preacher. The hero turns the people against him, and they hang him. The hero speculates that the preacher and his cohorts--who had assumed his appearance--had delved into old, forbidden religions and cults, until sadism and brutality became their fundamentals of faith. Even the blurb writer was inspired to one of his best efforts, by this taut reference.

Strange Murder-Driven Creatures Prowl the Evil
Apocalypse of a Weird Storm

From these examples, it appears that much of Burks' output took a supernatural turn. These were more or less random selections, mentioned because they happen to be fine efforts. Let me put it this way. His better stories seem to have been in the supernatural vein. Nor were they all mood pieces. "Six Doors to Horror," in TERROR TALES (March, 1935), is good old jolting abominableness, with a mysterious, shuttered house, doors that close by themselves, and malignant wind and water spirits. It has to do with a group of scoffing college youths who gather in an old Chinese house. The owner promises to show them something of his country's legends. But once unleased, the forces can't be controlled. In one macabre scene, one of the young men is drawn to a crypt, where a corpse is found, and where an evil entity commands it to bring a girl back for a spectral mating so the spirit's blood can be renewed.

The "speed merchant" tapered off during the forties and

fifties. He is now living in Pennsylvania with his wife. Today, Burks is better remembered for his working habits, rather than his works.

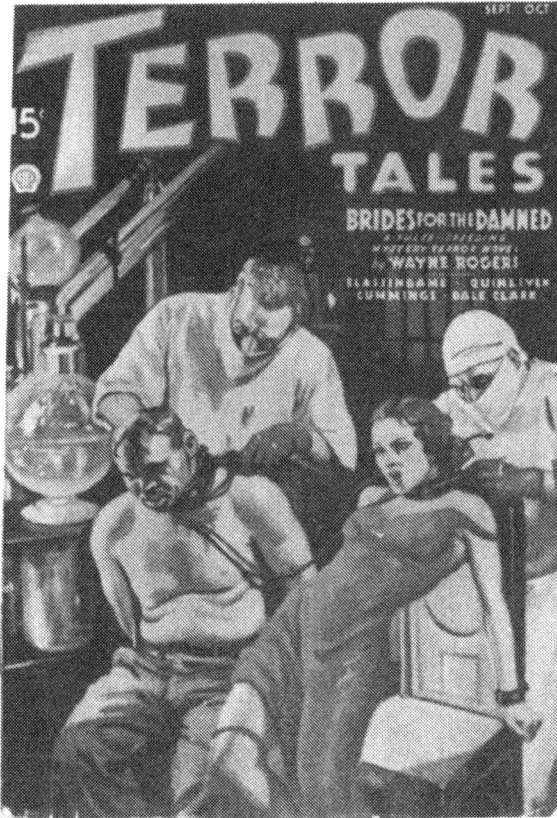

John Newton Howett's cover for the September-October, 1936 **Terror Tales** combines three distinctive and recurring visual elements in one scene: the heroine, of course, being mistreated, the mad doctor, and the slobbering monster, here more pacifistic than usual.

CHAPTER VIII. WEIRD FANTASY

> *Tales of horror find favor in times of depression, but lose their popularity as living conditions improve.*
>
> Ed Bodin

While on the subject of spectralism, let's see what other authors were doing in this line. You'll recall that a weird menace story was supposed to have a logical explanation. No matter how bizarre or outrageous the plot complications, everything was to be rationally resolved. At least, that's what editors were telling their authors. And story after story followed this concept. Many readers, whose appetites had been whetted for a few juicy vampires or werewolves, must have felt let down when the mysterious fiend was unmasked as a conniving uncle, mad inventor or disbarred doctor.

As one lady wrote in 1936: "I think that the most terrifying things are the things nobody understands. I don't like to have the villains always turn out to be just mean old men going around in masks."

Another reader commented the same year: "Why don't you give us more stories of the supernatural, without any physical explanation? Something that leaves you hanging, gives you a chance to ponder, even after you've turned in for the night?"

Well, the funny thing is, that's just what the magazines had been giving them. It was in small doses, granted. But if they had been paying attention, they would have remembered some noteworthy efforts in this direction. For despite editorial admonitions to explain all the ghost-like goings-on, authors found many opportunities to sidestep this obligation. Much of the fantasy in these magazines appeared in the 1934-1938 period. Among fantasy authors of this period, both Wyatt Blassingame and Paul Ernst were consistently interesting. In each case, about a third of their output was in this vein, most of it for Popular Publications.

Now the covers have hit a lurid extreme, as all sorts of frightful tortures are perpetrated on the fair maidens, most of whom by now have been divested of their clothes. This later Howett, August-September, 1937, is a far cry from his early Gothic dungeon scenes.

Blassingame's "The Horror at His Heels," in HORROR STORIES (August-September, 1936) incorporates his first plot device. You'll remember that device called for the character fleeing from a menace. In fact, it also utilizes elements of the second device, that is, the protagonist menaced by walls closing in. In this case, though, the roles of the protagonist and menace are reversed. Briefly, a member of an archeology party excavating near a Mayan city finds a treasure map. An old brown-skinned man appears, who had "died before Spanish was spoken in the land of the Sun and Eagle." The protagonist tries to kill him, then flees to the catacombs. He races down the passageways. But each time he makes a turn, the corridor behind grows smaller. Finally, he's trapped. He can't move. The next day, the others find his body, buried between stones that hadn't been disturbed in five hundred years.

This author produced several fine examples. A conjurer who died a hundred years earlier returns to exact vengeance on the hero's family, and prevent any member from inheriting the estate. He employs gruesome means, seizing the hero's fiancee, and forcing her into a profane wedding ceremony involving corpses, as he reads from the Book of the Devil.

Two of Blassingame's recitals involve demoniac children. When a white man marries a native girl, her rejected suitor casts a spell on their child-to-be. The baby is born horribly deformed, and precociously develops into a monster, bent on killing its father. Even though the man escapes to civilization, the fate overtakes him. Reminiscent of this idea, another story tells of a man finding a strange child in a deserted bay area. His cook recognizes it; it seems that two years earlier, when it was three, the father cursed it when he learned it was the son of a neighbor, not his. Henceforth, anyone protecting

There's no way out for the protagonist, in Wyatt Blassingame's "The Horror at His Heels," which exemplifies one of the author's two main approaches to weird fiction. It appeared in **Horror Stories,** August-September, 1936.

it would die. (Apparently, Blassingame was fond of curses as a motivational factor.) The child ceased to grow after that. An unseen presence enters the house and murders the man. A friend takes the child and is likewise killed.

In a stunning short, he depicts a somber fate: A reporter prevails on his friend to take him into a forbidden opium den. There is a fight. and the friend saves the reporter's life at the cost of his own. Then the reporter is wounded, and nears death. He awakens on a plain of desolate flatness-- among the damned. The scene changes, and he sees his friend's body flung over the rail of a ship, followed by another body--his.

Ernst, too, turned out some effective fantasies. In "The Thing Behind the Iron Door," in HORROR STORIES (October-November, 1937), a couple rents an old house, in spite of the villagers' mutterings of a dire doom. In a rear cellar they find a great stone that can be moved aside. A passage takes them to a ledge around a pool, overlooked by a monstrous metal statue, recognized as the Indra of the Mayans, the rain god. It is made of gold. At one point, on the hidden steps, they feel the "pressure of something black and unseen creeping past us. . ." There is a villainous real estate agent, who covets the wife, and plans to drive the couple mad, and some unexplained phenomena: the idol crashing over and killing him, and a freak downpour of rain, that began when the rain god tipped over.

The blurb for his "Man Into Monster," in TERROR TALES (August, 1935) called it "A Novelette of Ghastly Evil." The hero visits his sweetheart, to find her father, an Egyptologist, suffering from a peculiar malady that is transforming him into an ape. The glandular regression is accompanied by severe pain. The evil culprit behind it is the professor's assistant, obsessed with the heroine. He causes the ailment through effigies and an ancient ritual, and uses it against the hero. But the hero turns the tables when he finds the figures of himself and the professor, and then uses the same method against the villain, to make him reverse the process and thus save the professor and himself.

The closest Ernst came to repeating a theme was in a few selections incorporating the idea of the murderer punished indirectly through his victim. For instance, when a man murders his old father and buries him under a cherry tree, the tree starts to die. This goads him into a fury, and he tries to chop it down. A branch clutches him and the ax slips and kills him. Later, the tree recovers. A man kills his uncle by holding his nose and mouth, and forcing water into his lungs. Then he finds himself unable to swallow any water; his body even rejects intravenous injections. Finally, a blood vessel bursts and he dies. Through a geometric crystal he's fashioned, a man sees into another dimension. He discovers that his best friend has deceived him with his wife. He entices the friend into the world beyond, then kills him. But the body remains attracted to his, and follows him back, where it stays by his side, unseen except when viewed through the crystal.

It's not surprising that so many examples of the supernatural appeared under the Ernst byline. He was a frequent contributor to WEIRD TALES, and had shown a predilection in this direction early in his career. He was born in 1900. His first WEIRD TALES story appeared in 1928, but he didn't get into writing full-time until he was 30. He had traveled before, to such places as North Africa, Yugoslavia, Germany and Spain. He wrote on the side until payments for stories equalled his office salary.

"For no reason that I can think of," he recently commented, "I began with weird and supernatural stories." A success in this line was the Dr. Satan series, eight stories in WEIRD TALES in the mid-thirties, about "the world's weirdest criminal," who has to contend with Ascott Keane, one of fiction's most unusual detectives. For some reason, he says, he dreamed about half of his weird narratives, so explicitly, "that when I woke up in the morning I had a story as complete as though dictated to me. Unfortunately, this never worked for anything but far-out stuff; standard yarns such as I did later had to be whittled out laboriously."

Standard yarns, you say? Some might contend there was no such thing in the pulps. As for Ernst, his material showed a craftsmanship and attention to detail that set it apart from

The only trouble with fun like this is that it's over with so fast. This cover is from the September-October, 1937 **Terror Tales.** From the mid-1937's to the forties, covers on Popular's **Horror** and **Terror** pulps showed the heroines being tortured (or dispatched) in various ingenious ways.

the work of many others. Unlike most of his "blood brothers," he avoided excessive violence and lurid murders, for the most part. In 1939, Ernst submitted his own hero-of-the-month contribution. Super heroes were popular then, with the likes of DOC SAVAGE, THE SHADOW, G-8, THE SPIDER, THE PHANTOM DETECTIVE and others. His entry was THE AVENGER (now being reissued in paperback), under the Kenneth Robeson house name, the super crime fighter who eschewed killing. He only stunned the baddies with his unerring marksmanship. Today, Ernst lives in Florida, where Blassingame, Frederick C. Davis, Hugh B. Cave, all former mystery-terror pulpsters, have retired.

One of the most effective short pieces in a Popular publication appeared in 1934, in TERROR TALES. "If Thy Right Hand Offend Thee," by the English author, John Flanders, has the succinct economy of a John Collier. It is a vivid account of retribution and redemption. A jeweler sees a hand reaching through his doorway and drops the heavy steel shutter, severing it. It crawls into his shop and eludes him for awhile until he can grab it and discard it. Later, his business fails, and his own hand takes on the ugly and discolored appearance of the other one. He is reduced to begging. One night, he finds a shop still open, rushes to it and thrusts his hand under a descending shutter, which slices it off. When he's recovered, he finds his old strength back and knows that his shrewd business sense is as sharp as ever.

An unusual vignette appeared under the Robert C. Blackmon name (a pseudonym for Roger Howard Norton), "Our Grave Is Waiting" in HORROR STORIES (July, 1936), a ghost story with pathos. A member of an engineering party in an Arizona ghost town wanders into the Palace Saloon one night, and finds a gathering of people who had died a century earlier. He falls in love with Rose, a girl with a bright red rose in her black hair, and a "weird, brumal chill flowing from her white flesh."

Despite the sordidness of this situation, in Paul Ernst's "Man Into Monster," **Terror Tales,** August, 1935, there is just a mention in the text about lusting monsters stripping defenseless damsels. Ernst did not go in for lurid details, which, of course, did not discourage the graphic efforts.

Most of the regular contributors to the weird menace magazines avoided the dark byways of psychic phenomena, even some who wrote fantasies for other publications, such as Hugh B. Cave and Arthur Leo Zagat. Others strayed infrequently, such as Wayne Rogers. One of his rare examples is found in MYSTERY ADVENTURES (July, 1936). "Buried Alive" concerns a wife who is bored with her husband, and has become involved with the owner of a strange house. It was left to him after his eccentric uncle died; the old man had kept it closed after being jilted by his sweetheart forty years before. The house exerts a mesmeric influence over the woman, and gains control over its owner, driving him to try to entomb her alive. Her husband saves her and later, they discover a cubicle, within which is a skeleton, the girl who had spurned the uncle, and who had been walled up to die by him. It was the uncle's evil will which controlled the nephew.

It wasn't so much that you questioned the why of these depradations—after all, anyone who looked like these uglies just had to enjoy others' sufferings—but the how. How did such fright faces as on this December, 1937 - January, 1938 cover entice so many fair young things into their clutches in the first place?

That most versatile of authors, John H. Knox, was another who rarely dealt in supernaturalism. He did at least once, in THRILLING MYSTERY, which likewise, stayed away from this type of story, to a great extent. "Horses of Death" (July, 1936) has to do with a ghostly cavalry, a murdered boy whose body is hidden beneath an old mulberry tree, where his fiancee's grandmother had waited in vain for the return of her Rebel soldier. There the girl goes, and is avenged when the murderer is struck down by a horseman in the sky, her lover come back for her.

Another THRILLING MYSTERY representation, "You Hang for Murder," by Jack D'Arcy (October, 1936) bears a strong affinity to W. F. Harvey's superb "August Heat." An artist, involved with another man's wife, is thinking of her one day in his studio, and subconsciously sketches a man hanging from a gallows, his face stamped with agony and remorse. On the street, later, he sees the man of the gallows. He follows him to a stonecutter's; there he is found working on a tombstone. It has the artist's name and date of birth, and date of death for that day. He goes home to await his fate. Soon, the husband of the woman arrives, who is the stonecutter.

One more mention from the same magazine. In the June 1937 issue, Carl Jacobi's "Satan's Kite" makes use of one of the author's favorite settings: the Malay Archipelago. A British conservator of forests in Borneo with his wife and daughter is being menaced in a most unusual way. He had stolen a piece of rare silk from a forbidden temple in India. It is supposed to have mystic properties. For his crime, his wife is made to suffer a wasting-away, her condition waxing and waning as a kite flying in the forest nearby rises and falls. When it settles to the ground, she dies. Next, his daughter becomes afflicted, as another kite is seen above the trees.

The Britisher's friend attempts to destroy the kite while still in the air by shunting flammable gun cotton up the wire to it. The burning mass falls on the ill-fated man and kills him.

In its brief run, ACE MYSTERY averaged three fantasies an issue, certainly a high proportion for a non-occult publication. One may well be among the most effective vampire stories to appear in the pulps. I'm speaking of "Coyote Woman," by Charles Marquis Warren (July, 1936), the same issue with the Knox story. No mist-shrouded, moldering, bat-haunted castle here, with enigmatic, wraith-like shapes creeping about. Instead, there's a desert, the hot, burning sand emphasizing the inflamed blood-lust of a terrifying trio of the undead. The doom here is as overpowering as in Arthur Burks' "Devils in the Dust."

They come upon a man struggling to survive, after his mules and supplies have disappeared. There are three frightful apparitions: two cowboys with faces like beasts--"snapping black eyes, huge canine nostrils, coarsely matted hair"--and a woman with an ominously beautiful face with full, red lips and strangely lacklustre red eyes.

Like jackals fighting over a piece of meat, they fall on him. The woman interposes herself, and in spite of his pain-wracked, exhausted state, he still responds to her mesmeric allure.

"The woman's face was close to his. Through swollen, cracked lips he gasped, 'Give me some water!'

"The red eyes mocked him without light in them. She shook her head. 'There is no water, Halloran.'

" 'The bargain--water--'

"Jed and Larn roared. Their horrible canine faces came closer. Their eyes snapped greedily, hungrily.

" 'Water thins blood,' Larn rumbled. 'We don't want it thin!' "

This Amos Sewell rendering for Whipple's "Curse of the Harcourts," in **Dime Mystery**, March, 1935, is pure weird menace: the evil nemesis bending over the helpless heroine, raised knife in hand, while the bound hero struggles futilely. But the story itself is far, far above such conventionalities—an outstanding example of imaginative horror.

They attack him once more, then fight over him. He's saved in the nick of time when the rising sun forces the monsters into their nearby graves, where he is able to kill them.

Let's move back to Popular for a final assessment. Here is one of the most remarkable extended pieces of imaginative fiction to appear during the thirties. DIME MYSTERY in 1935 printed a six-part tightly strung saga of a self-sustaining curse that bridges nine hundred years, five countries and three continents--the curse of the Harcourts. Unheralded--it never even received mention on the covers--and now forgotten, the series had three attributes: good plotting, dramatic intensity, and--a rarity in the pulps--character development.

The author was Chandler H. Whipple, never a prolific type, but certainly, a careful one. After working for Clayton, he served as an editor at Popular, and was with the company at this time. The next year he left to become editor of Munsey's ARGOSY, taking over when Jack Byrne left.

In the first episode, Signor Pirelli from Florence is a guest of the d'Harcourt family, in Norman France in the year one thousand. That night, he attempts to rape his host's daughter, and is beaten off by the servants. As he leaves, he puts a curse on the family and its ancestral line. The baron and baroness later fall into his power, and die from fearful tortures. Their daughter is saved. "Curse of the Harcourts" (March, 1935), the second instalment, may be a highpoint, although it is hard to single out any one section. Two hundred years have passed. The present Baron Henry d'Harcourt has settled in Wales, with his bride, Gwendolyn. There he incurs the wrath of a Druid priest and his followers.

But it is not only the believers in Hu and Keridwen with whom he must contend. There is Mata Sim, a Hindu leper ostensibly faithful to the family. In reality, he is the reincarnation of Signor Pirelli. Mata Sim abducts Gwendolyn, at the same time the Druids prepare to sacrifice Henry. To appease their pagan gods, he offers to descend through the cauldron of the priestess of Annwy, the abode of the dead. Only King Arthur and seven out of one thousand had ever returned from that dread place, he learns. He faces a transcendent test of endurance and faith, as he slowly makes his way down into the bowels of the earth.

"There was an arched bridge across this chasm, but in its center, blocking the way, was a thing far more horrible than all that lay below. He knew no words that would describe this hulking, fang-mouthed monster whose fingers were claws and whose legs twined down to the bottom of hell. . .Yet it

Another fun and games session is in full swing, on this cover for the January-February, 1938 issue. In late 1937, **Horror** and **Terror** ceased carrying cover artist credit, as well as the names of the interior illustrators.

had a human face, and he knew that he should know this face, that someone back in his dim ancestral past was calling its name to him."

There is a final shattering struggle with this demon of the depths, the monster who guards the bridge of hell--the underworld spirit of Mata Sim.

The third part takes place during the plague of London. Robert d'Harcourt fights an evil entity in a black cloak, Pirelli again; both he and his wife contract the plague and nearly die. They exorcise the vengeful spirit, again winning a temporary respite for the family.

The doom follows the Harcourts to Florence, in the year 1532 and then to Puritan New England, where John Harcourt and his wife, Elizabeth, have settled, and finally, to the present. Lionel, the last of the line, comes to a final reckoning with Pirelli as he awaits his death after receiving a message that the curse is going to kill him.

This series was the closest thing to a serial Popular ran in its weird menace line. In fact, it was the only connected work to appear there. Editorial policy forbade the use of continuations. The idea was to run only complete stories, perhaps due to a fear that readers would not buy the publication in the middle of something, or would not want to wait for it to end. Since both HORROR STORIES and TERROR TALES were on bi-monthly schedules the policy made sense.

On the creative level, Whipple's series provided effective atmospheric touches and at times, exalted descriptive passages. Here are two random selections.

Really, there's no reason for the poor woman to be nude; she has enough other problems as it is, in Whipple's "A Child for Satan," in **Dime Mystery**, September, 1935, part of the "Harcourt" series.

• They were strange eyes, like none he had ever seen before, and he could not look away. He seemed to be looking into unfathomable depths as he stared into them, beholding the silent answer to all the questions of the universe, though why, he could not fathom. Seeking the answer, he felt that all his being was sinking into the eyes, that the bottomless depths were swallowing his soul. And feeling this, he knew something akin to fear.

"You are Lucia?" he said at last.

"Yes," she answered. Her voice was the tinkling of tiny silver bells, yet there was in it a rhythm as slow and fearful and eternal as the dark Arno's roll. "You are to come with me."

• I think that all the world is dead. . .Now there is the chill dread which heralds his approach. I wonder if I am going to be brave. Now I hear the rustle and the soft footsteps which I heard when the priest was here. He is coming. . .

He is here. . .! Like a chill wind he enters my body! Like a stormy sea his soul sweeps over mine!

At the reader level, the series generated some down-to-earth commendations. "Those stories by Chandler H. Whipple are absolutely the nuts. This is the kind I have been looking for everywhere." And another reader asked, "When are you going to start another series? The one by Whipple is swell. It gives the reader something definite to look forward to."

The answer, of course, was never.

CHAPTER IX. BATTLE AT THE NEWSSTANDS

Those were the times when we sold as fast as we could write. The markets were tremendous. The pulps were magnificent, not altogether for their content, but because they were a breeding ground and a learning place for beginning writers. When a pulp writer came to do a screenplay, for instance, he knew what scenes were, how a story must progress, how introspection slowed the action. And he could tell the story.

William R. Cox

These days Madison Avenue would chuckle at the modest circulation figures and unprepossessing financial statements of the pulps. Yet thirty-five years or so ago, sales in the neighborhood of two hundred to three hundred thousand copies of an issue meant a fair profit to a publisher. He thought in terms of thousands--and sometimes, hundreds--not millions.

In this heady environment, survival depended on newsstand sales. Mail subscriptions accounted for maybe five percent of the copies placed in customers' hands. Who wanted to mount an extensive mail solicitation campaign, or bother with return cards inserted in copies, or even subscription forms? It was much easier to stick on a bright, garish cover and let that do the work for you. And advertising? You couldn't expect much there--probably around ten percent of your revenue. No, the battlefield was the newsstand, where the gaudy covers slugged it out with each other for the customer's dime. It was a fight to the (coated) finish. Publishers scanned newsstand sales returns as ardently as television producers today agonize over the latest viewer ratings.

It wasn't just story ideas or treatment that publishers copied, as can be seen by the March, 1938 cover here, and the **Dime Mystery** cover that follows. The scenes are so similar, there's no doubt one inspired the other . . . all just part of the battle for newsstand notice that publishers conducted.

Dime Mystery's "editorial page" was called Dark Council in early issues.

The watchword was, sell out the counter copies. That's why some titles only came out every other month; this gave them twice as much time as the monthlies to find a taker. There's a story of a publisher of a western magazine, who doggedly made the rounds of the New York newsstands, rubber-stamping the next month's date on unsold copies of his publication.

Remember the low pay pulp editors received? You know why, of course. The pulps walked a thin line between profit and loss. Here's what a typical issue might cost. Let's say the press run was 125,000 copies, total pages, 128 and the average size, six and three-quarters by nine and three-quarters, with four-color cover, naturally, and priced at ten cents. Printing would cost about a cent a copy. Authors' rates would average more than a half cent a copy, based on a penny a word for approximately sixty-five thousand words an issue. (Some authors probably would be getting more than a cent a word.) Then there were the office operating

costs, plus freight and distribution. And of course, the newsstand dealer got a percentage of each copy sold. Those not
sold were a complete loss to the publisher. His return on
each copy sold came to about five cents each. To break
even, he had to sell from sixty to eighty thousand copies. If
he could sell a hundred thousand, he stood to make better
than a thousand dollars. As a matter of fact, a hundred
thousand was considered a norm, but for class circulation,
such as ATLANTIC, HARPER'S, and FORTUNE, which of
course, sold above the ten-cents-a-copy scale of most pulps.

So the trick was to sell at least a hundred thousand, the
more the better. It wasn't easy to do, though. Many titles
sold in the neighborhood of sixty to eighty thousand copies
each, some even lower. But there was a way around this
problem. That was to develop a chain of magazines. Obviously, it was a lot more economical to print several titles,
and spread many of the costs around, than to concentrate on
only one title. Then, too, you could attract authors easier.
They would figure on being able to sell to one outlet, if not
another.

To add to the vagaries of success, sometimes, it was as easy
to start on a shoestring in pulp publishing as it had been to
buy stocks on margin before the crash. An editor once
observed: "All you need is some credit from a dealer in pulp
paper and from a printer, and an arrangement with a distribution company. You can promise to pay authors after
publication. You can pay the printing and paper bills when
the check for sold copies comes in from the distributor." In
other words, you could put yourself into instant business,
accept stories from struggling authors eager for a chance to
break into print, and willing to live on promises, publish and
distribute a batch of magazines, fail to make costs, and go
bankrupt--all without a cent of money changing hands.

Some publishers paid on publication. These were the strugglers trying to make ends meet. The established companies, like Popular and Thrilling, paid on acceptance. Popular's word rate generally started at one cent a word. Henry Steeger has noted that some authors received as much as five cents a word (very few, undoubtedly). Thrilling paid a cent a word. Hubbard's company (which published MYSTERY ADVENTURES) paid two-fifths to three-fifths cents a word. The Spicies paid promptly, at rates from one to one and a half cents a word. Wyn's company offered from a half to a cent a word and paid on acceptance. This whole business of authors' rates had stabilized, by the thirties, at a cent a word. But earlier, the pulps paid more. In the twenties, authors made from two to five cents a word, generally. Those were the days when Max Brand was getting ten cents a word.

It was at that time that two publishers, mainly, had the field to themselves: Munsey and Street & Smith. The American News Company distributed Street & Smith publications to some 100,000 newsstands each month. Then came a day when Street & Smith pulled out, leaving American News with no other pulps. So the distributor encouraged its publishers to bring out pulp lines of their own. New titles began appearing. Soon, no one was selling enough to make a good return. This resulted in lowered author rates, which finally leveled off at the familiar penny a word.

But, in spite of these niggardly word rates (which, incidentally, have been perpetuated right up to the present in some publications), an enterprising soul could turn them to his profit without any more effort than it took to correct punctuation and sign his name. At least, it was possible, even if the following attempt happened to end in failure. The account is taken from the AMERICAN MERCURY (March, 1936). The contributor of the article signed it, Anonymous.

He wrote:

"I was actually one of the writers in a strange literary chain which has since become a famous gag, to be included in the "pulp play" that every pulpster dreams of writing some day. A friend telephoned me one afternoon and offered a cent and a half a word if I would deliver a story to him by three o'clock the following afternoon, so that he could send it to his regular two-cent-a-word market later in the day. By the time I had the plot worked out in my mind, my wife returned with some friends who were to spend the evening.

"So I phoned another pulpster, offering a cent and a quarter, if he would write a story for me by two o'clock the following afternoon. He agreed but became involved with convivial companions and phoned still another writer, promising one cent flat if delivery of the manuscript was made by noon. For some reason this man gave up the job and at midnight telephoned the original writer with a three-quarter-cent offer. The creator of the chain had some fiery and uncomplimentary words for the lot of us, but he sat down at his typewriter and wrote the piece himself before morning."

While newsstand sales were the lifeblood of pulp publishing, advertising could be a shot in the arm. The publisher depended on ads for his inside front, and inside and outside back covers, as well as some on other pages. These represented additional welcome revenue, certainly. They were sold for groups of publications. That is, the same ad would appear in all the pulps in a group the same month. Thus, while one pulp might only have a circulation of something like fifty thousand (hardly an impressive figure for the advertiser's purposes), the total circulation for the group of magazines might be a million or more.

Circulation strength, of course, determined the price the

publisher could get for an ad page. Popular's group of pulps, for instance, frequently averaged better than a million and sometimes close to two million sales a month. So the company could set its rate card higher than its competitors. Popular charged as much as $1520 for a full-page black and white ad inside, and $4000 for the back cover, which was in full color. A company like Wyn's Ace group, on the other hand, with far less total circulation, charged around $500 for a black and white ad.

Few pulp groups in the thirties carried monthly advertising billings over $5000. Publishers felt fortunate to sell the three covers without some kind of deal. Compare this return to "slick" advertising then. A black and white page in GOOD HOUSEKEEPING--circulation nearly two million-- cost $6000, while the back cover went for more than $10,000.

The May, 1938 **Dime Mystery** looks very much like the **Thrilling Mystery** cover of two months earlier, except that as was typical of each publica- tion, the gal is nude on one, and fully dressed, except for one errant strap, on the other.

Street & Smith was the giant of the twenties. Then, it had a guaranteed paid circulation for nine titles of 1.2 million. But by the thirties, it had slipped, losing its position to Popular. In 1936, Popular listed a total of thirteen magazines for advertising purposes. Actually, the company put out a few more than that, but those were the stable titles. Total circulation (according to figures from both *N. W. Ayer's* and *Standard Rate and Data Service*) came to about 1,500,000 a month. That year, an inside ad page cost $1,200 and the back cover, $3,900.

Street & Smith listed twelve pulps in its group that year; they had a combined circulation of 1.1 million. An inside ad cost $1,050, and the back cover, $3,200.

The third of the "big three," the Thrilling group, with ten magazines, topped Street & Smith's circulation then by 55,000. A page cost $1,000, and the back cover went for $3,600.

Here are statistics on some of the other pulp companies of that period. The Newsstand Fiction group of nine titles, including MYSTERY ADVENTURES and BLACK MASK, had 600,000 circulation, and charged for the respective pages, $400 and $1500. Magazine Publishers, which carried SECRET AGENT X and ACE MYSTERY, among its nine titles, had 640,000 circulation, and charged $550 and $2,000, respectively. The Spicies--Mystery, Detective, Adventure, Western--with PRIVATE DETECTIVE, reached 379,000 customers. We don't know what their advertising rates were, since they weren't listed.

And finally, an indication of things to come: In 1936 POPULAR COMICS, with 150,000 circulation for the one title, sold its cover for $475. It wouldn't be long before the comic books would be nudging the pulps off the stands, at the same time they attracted the advertisers to them.

Throughout the thirties, Popular led the other pulp publishers, including those not mentioned in this circulation survey, such as Dell, Fiction House, Warner Publications and Munsey. The company reached a high in audited circulation in 1937, with more than 1,866,000 for sixteen titles. What all these figures added up to was a $25 million dollar business, involving some thirteen hundred writers and 130 or so pulp titles, read by some 30 million people a month.

The title, The River Styx, replaced Dark Council, in **Dime Mystery** in 1936.

CHAPTER X. FROM THE ESOTERIC TO THE EROTIC

*The story of horror depends very largely
for its effect upon the author's treatment of
material phenomena; the sex novel also, in its
different metier, is concerned with material-
istic aspects. There is an essential relation
between horror and passion.*
                    E. H. Visiak
                    THE 19th CENTURY (July, 1936)

Probably you're thinking that by now, the mystery-terror
magazines must have run out of nasty subjects. But as far as
the shudder pulps were concerned, you couldn't have too
much of a bad thing. As they entered their sex-sadistic
phase (around mid-1937), they got even more explicit. Now
the authors were shedding many of their earlier circumlocu-
tions in favor of a punchier delivery. And new authors were
injecting new blood in the proceedings (no pun intended).
The cover illustrations provide a visual record of the newly
emerging style.
  Earlier, issues depicted the heroines fleeing staring-eyed,
knife-wielding madmen. Their dresses often were not even
disarrayed. There was little eroticism to the scenes. But in
1937, the nude look was in. Now the heroines were being

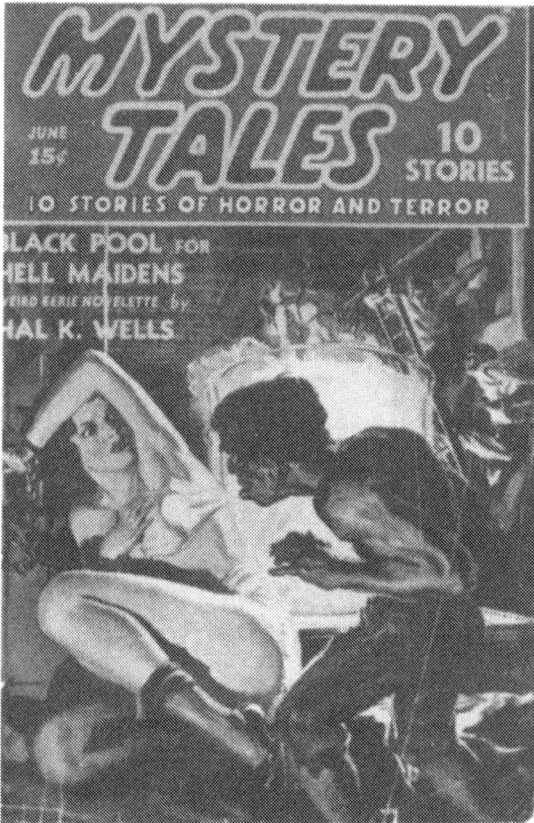

This cover (another Saunders charmer) and the following are typical of the sadistic eroticism promoted by the Red Circles. Ordinarily, the covers did not illustrate a story, but in this case, June, 1938, the scene is from Cyril Plunkett's "Fear's Fiancees."

tortured in a more sophisticated manner, if that's the term, by such contrivances as buzzsaws, boiling (and freezing) water, electric drills, and knife-edged corsets. The deranged look in the fiends' eyes had been replaced by one of depravity. For Popular Publications, which was leading the way in these changes, it was a matter of clearing away the cobwebs of decay and oiling the creaking door of the company's house of horrors. The covers thus gained a polish that even today look modern. Inside, the contents, for the most part, emphasized more action, less reaction.

Although sex was rearing its head, as they say, it didn't mean that suddenly all restraint had been cast aside. (In recent years, some commentators have taken a superficial look and declared mistakenly that these pulps promoted every kind of perversion imaginable.) Actually, the pulps, of all story markets, displayed a diffidence and caution which was often exasperating. They just didn't want to come to grips with raw passion. You would have to search assiduously to find undue amounts of prurience, salaciousness or obscenity, to borrow definitions popularized by our modern Supreme Court, although every once in awhile something sizzled.

This is the paradox of the pulps. As the "blue collars" bible of reading pleasure, so to speak, they catered to an unsophisticated and unsubtle class, to generalize a bit. These readers demanded hard-hitting fiction without frills and literary pretensions. The pulps delivered this. But at the same time, they steered clear of forthright sexual explication. Instead, they dealt in euphemisms. Often, the writing was repressively ambiguous. "A fate worse than death," and variations of this, cropped up frequently, for instance. Even the swear words were mild--with hell and damn, about the only two used, appearing as explanation rather than exclamation.

Of course, there was a reason, or rather, several reasons, for this state of affairs. Pulps which used the mails had to observe a considerable degree of decorum, or else run afoul of postal inspectors. Because they were mass-oriented, like television today, they tried not to offend their readers. And as escape literature, they paid more attention to creating their own never-never lands of mystery and romance, than to scrupulous fidelity to life. However, all of this didn't stop some pulp publishers from straddling the self-censorship fence. Popular opened its pages to a freer, more outspoken presentation. There were others who went beyond that.

An example from Popular pulps separated by four years shows the changes time wrought. The comparison is between two stories that feature a young man and his wife, in both cases, victims of lust-besotted creatures who glory in inflicting pain, as the blurbs might have put it.

Nat Schachner's "Monsters of the Pit" in TERROR TALES (November 1934), finds the couple honeymooning in the Canadian northern wilderness. Man-beasts drag them to an underground lair. There a priest with putty-like skin and bulging forehead (the inevitable disguise, again), rules over them. He prepares to torture the bride; he slashes off her clothes while the Neanderthalers exultantly caper and cavort. But the moment of truth never arrives. Before the sacrificial victim can let out one good blood-curdling whoop, the hero breaks free, unmasks the villain, and escapes with his wife, both none the worse for their experience.

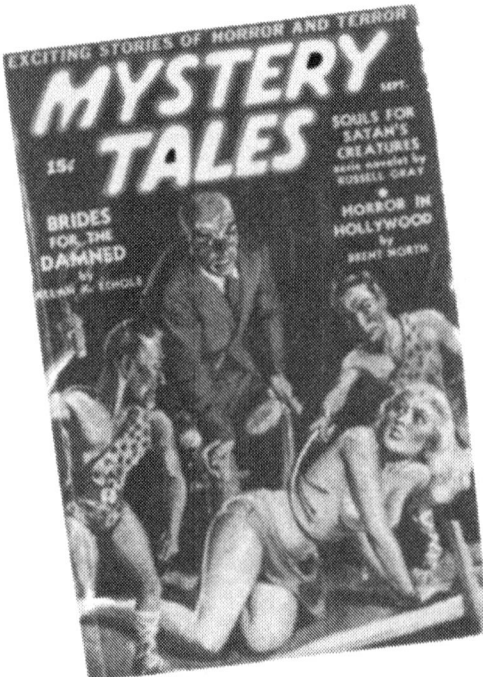

September, 1939

Now then, we move ahead to Russell Gray's "Burn--Lovely Lady!" in DIME MYSTERY (June, 1938). This time, depravity is depicted graphically. The situation is similar: a young man and his bride are to be tortured. The experience turns into an anguished test of endurance. This time there is little equivocation. For Schachner's primordial, mindless myrmidons, substitute a clache of cackling, obscene-minded old men and women. And for the involved and sometimes stilted writing, substitute crackling, biting prose. The man's wife must submit willingly to pain for two hours, to win freedom for herself and her husband. She agrees. The ringleader, an old crone, inserts a needle slowly through her breast, and into other tender parts of her body. She then stretches her by chains operated by a windlass, and has her flogged. Each time her victim faints, she revives her by an injection.

So we see a contrast between the overstatement of the early years, and the economy of the later period, between prolixity and specificity. From Schachner's story: "The whole phantasmagoria had fallen into a sinister pattern, infinitely horrible in its implications. . .He shouted strange oaths in a voice he did not recognize as his own; he clamored frantically against the rising roar of the quake." The arch-fiend is termed a "minister of suffering," an inappropriate title, besides being a contrived one.

On the other hand, Gray keeps to a minimum luridness for luridness' sake. His straight description remains unencumbered with the colorful adjectives that served so many authors earlier. His tormentor is simply, "the old woman." His scenes come alive, as pain becomes a palpable thing for the reader. "She probed Joyce's body with her skeleton-like hands, and I could see Joyce's flesh crawl. . .Tor's tiny eyes popped and saliva drooled from the corners of his mouth. . .I saw the muscles of her arms and thighs and waist cord with the strain of trying to hold her feet from the fire. . .And still she did not cry out. . .''

In keeping with the earlier prevailing attitude of calling a spade an implement for digging, one of the authors from the Gothic period explains the fate worse than death the villain plans for the heroine. A revolting creature nearby impatiently paws the ground and oggles her. She's to be given to him. " 'When she has suffered through hunger and thirst and pain till she can suffer no more, they will be married,' the villain promises." In other words, it's going to be all perfectly legal, you see. But within a few years, such vagueness gave way to more direct treatment. Gray, again, minces no words in saying that girls are being tortured into accepting a life of prostitution. The more outspoken "rape," "ravished" and "possessed" had by then replaced such earlier evasions as "awful lust" and "fearful fate."

Russell Gray's prose epitomizes the new look of the late thirties. In some ways, he proved a dominant force of the period. Like Norvell Page, he worked on newspapers where, if nothing else, a writer learns to be concise. His stories, like Page's, generated excitement, but not in as slambang a way. He sold his first story, "The Cat Woman," for sixty dollars to Popular Publications in 1936. From a penny a word, he went to one and a half cents. His first year he earned two thousand dollars, enough to quit his job and freelance. "When in 1937 I abandoned newspaper work for pulp fiction, I found the horror-terror market wide open and on the whole, paying as "high rates" (by which term editors mean rates not lower than) as more sedate detective magazines," he notes in WRITER'S DIGEST (July, 1945). In the next four years, he turned out "two million words of horror and terror and sold every word I wrote." Yes, there were a few pulp authors who seemed to sell everything they wrote, even though it's hard to believe.

In the forties, Gray began working the detective markets. They proved tougher, he found, when his first five stories bounced. Before long, though, he was producing and selling consistently. He moved out of pulps into hardboiled hardbacks, under his own name, Bruno Fischer, shortly after. Recently, Fischer has been in the administrative end of book publishing.

Before moving on to other publications, suppose we glance at a few more examples from Popular. Since Schachner drew some uncomplimentary remarks, we ought to update him and see how he does. Some of his early works were good. But by 1937 he had pruned his style of much of the stifling deadwood, and it was healthier for it. His "Children of Murder" in DIME MYSTERY that year builds up effectively to a crisis, as the hero and heroine investigate fiery deaths caused by fiendish children.

"The shopkeeper made no move. His eyes burned on my wife. 'No one,' he whispered dryly, 'leaves the store of old Jem until he buys.'

'That's what you think,' I retorted with a creditable amount of sarcasm, and strode to the door. I reached for the knob. There was none. I dug my fingers furiously into the crack between door and jamb, tugged. The door did not budge."

And what of that arch-Gothiciser of the thirties, Arthur Leo Zagat? Apparently, it was too much to hope that he would break his female-viewpoint habit. He didn't. But he modernized, too. His later stories moved along at a brisk pace, usually, and didn't exasperate the reader with rationalizations and introspections every page.

"Girls for the Spider Men," TERROR TALES (September-October, 1938), shifts its viewpoint, but repeatedly returns to the heroine. In this one, the villain masquerades as a gigantic spider, in a lair to which he brings girls. They are bound in sticky, weblike prisons, to be tortured by rich old men willing to pay for their perverted entertainment. In this and other stories by Zagat, there is now little reflection, unlike a few years earlier.

During this period, an occasional reincarnation of the Hairless Thing can be found. Only now, the accent is on venery, not viciousness. Thus, a scaly monster (uh huh, another disguise) gets worked up over one of his fair victims, at one point. His technique may have been crude, but he got results.

"Puffy, scaled hands were wandering with hellish deliberation over the girl's unclothed body. . .

" 'She doesn't realize the glorious thing that's awaiting her,' Harry whispered, as though confiding some glad secret. 'It's an honor to serve the Master that way. They sort of go mad after he begins. They go mad and enjoy it even more than we do--before they die.'

"The hell-spawned abomination was crouching ever lower over the girl, and I could see the frog-like lips, hinged like a toy animal's, working up and down at her throat in a travesty of nuptial kisses."

But "hell-spawned abominations" like this were infrequent. Emphasis now was on women, in particular, possessed of strange forces, under the sway of strange maladies, driven to dark deeds. By way of passing, two Wayne Rogers stories in 1937 point up this trend. They were "The Mummy Pack Prowls Again," and "Beast-Women Stalk at Night." In one, a horrible affliction turns young, healthy women into shriveled, shrunken creatures who in a frenzy rend the flesh from their victims. In the other, tawny shapes, nude ravening women, lope after their victims with the ferociousness of

THE GARGOYLES of MADNESS

by Russell Gray

Author of "Daughters of Lusting Torment," etc.

It was the tiny figurine of a repulsive naked female squatting on her heels, flabby breasts dangling, hands clasped over an obscenely swelling belly, hideous face contorted into an idiot smirk of slobbering bestiality. It was that—and final proof of the mad horror that stalked ruthlessly among the city's multi-millionaires!

Russell Gray's "Gargoyles of Madness," in **Uncanny Tales,** August, 1939, shows the favorite Red Circle predicament: the victims being whipped or otherwise tortured. When he wanted to, Gray could turn on sex-sadism as well (or bad) as anyone.

wolves, as the inhabitants cower in fear of an epidemic of lycanthropy. Naturally, a culprit is behind the dirty work: in one case, venting his hate on the town for ostracizing his father, in the other, trying to make everyone leave so he can later clean up with a vacation development.

So plot-wise, nothing much had changed over the years. Murder was still mysterious. Weird menaces still perpetrated it. But they did go about their business differently. Now they took time to philander a bit. And they were a lot nastier to women.

The year Popular began modifying its product--that is, 1937--new publications turned their steps in the same direction. What with ACE MYSTERY fizzling out after but three issues the year before, you'd think A. A. Wyn would have

Here is another full-fleshed Saunders heroine; the most provocative element of the otherwise unimaginative scene is the expanse of thigh shown. This was the cover of the August, 1937 **Eerie Stories,** a one-shot effort by Ace.

given up. But he came back with another mystery-terror entry, in an even feebler attempt to crack the field. It was EERIE STORIES, and it lasted one issue. The most exciting thing about it was the cover by Saunders–another of his alluring blondes. Unfortunately, Ace magazines often followed up these stimulating artistries with some of the poorest interior illustrations of just about any pulp, and this one was no exception. The magazine guaranteed "Startling Adventures in Chilling Horror." The individual story titles extended this duplicity: "Virgins of the Stone Death," "The Soul-Scorcher's Lair," "Her Isle of Horror," "Mate of the Beast," "The Pain Master's Bride." But the stories fell short, for the most part, of the magazine's lofty goal. "Virgins of the Stone Death" was about a criminal who feeds his followers hasheesh, and kills through an injection that causes near instantaneous rigor mortis. No, "The Pain Master's Bride" was not an example of matrimonial incompatibility. The "pain master" tortured victims with electricity to make them into life-like statues. "Mate of the Beast" was a reprint of "Wolf Vengeance" from ACE MYSTERY, with a new suggestive title.

Still not admitting defeat, Ace tried again the following year. This time it was EERIE MYSTERIES, probably with the expectation that the word, "Mystery," would put it over, even though ACE MYSTERY didn't make the grade two years earlier. Like EERIE STORIES, which it closely resembled, the new magazine sold for fifteen cents a copy. Some of the stories were picked up from Wyn's detective pulps, or from ACE MYSTERY again, for some element of violence, and retitled to sound worse than they were. Here are a few: "Horror's Handshake," "Abyss of the Wailing Dead," "Street of Ghouls," "Fangs of the Soul," "Satan's Ante-Chamber," "Modeled in Death." Four issues of the publication appeared, highlighting the works of such stellar luminaries as Ronald Flagg, Cliff Howe, Dennis Storm, Rexton Archer, Branton Black, Ralph Powers, Clifford Gray-- just about all house names, and as the policy was in such cases, good Anglo-Saxon derivations.

About this business of false names. Putting a name on the story other than the author's real one was a widespread practice in the pulps. There were several reasons. In some cases, authors took nom de plumes as a matter of course. We've seen how Bruno Fischer did not use his real name on his mystery-terror fiction, preferring Russell Gray. When an author had two stories in the same issue, the pseudonym avoided the obvious repetitiousness of the real name. Thus, Gray also used the name, Harrison Storm. Ray Cummings was also Ray King (after his middle name). The readers, of course, were not aware of this doubling up. In fact, readers sometimes preferred stories by one name over another, without realizing that both were the same writer. A controversy once flared in a western magazine over the merits of Max Brand as against George Owen Baxter, with the two factions unaware that they were the same person, or that both names were pseudonyms of Frederick Faust.

Most publishers employed house names--that grand and glorious contrivance that solved all sorts of problems. For instance, Popular Publications kept several handy; one in particular was very appropriate to the mystery-terror field: Emerson Graves. Then there was Raymond Whetstone, in Popular and Thrilling pulps. And what about that most perfect of all covers for an author with a second story in the same issue, the Spicy line's Justin Case? House names also served as subterfuges for reprinted stories, as well as authorship switches in series characters. Most of the super hero pulps--DOC SAVAGE, THE SPIDER, SECRET AGENT X, etc.--were written under house names. Say the author took sick. The publisher could bring someone else in for a while, and no one would know the difference. And yes, he could actually stoop so low as to use the house name as a club. Listen to this conversation between Mr. Penny-a-Word, the author, and Mr. Penny-Watcher, the publisher, on the unpleasant subject of word rates. (Note the abrupt ending.)

"You know, I've been turning out a fifty-five thousand-word novel every month for three years, Mr. Penny-Watcher. I've jammed every one with a cliff-hanging crisis every two pages, all kinds of daring exploits, and so many fiendish villains, I've lost count. We get letters from all around the country. Everybody likes it. So I think I should get more money for my work."

"Well now, Mr. Penny-a-Word, you know, Mr. Half-Cent-a-Word is anxious to try his hand at your series. He's willing to give me a novel a month for half the price. . ."

Unlike Wyn, who skirted the sex issue, Martin Goodman hit it head on in his Red Circle line. Goodman started from a hole in the wall in 1932, with westerns. By 1937, his Manvis Publications had fourteen titles and a guaranteed circulation close to five hundred thousand. Like Ace and Popular, Manvis--and its subsidiary, Western Fiction Publishing Company--featured a cover symbol: a red bullet with the words, "A Red Circle Magazine" around it. Today, his firm, Magazine Management Company, handles the highly lucrative Marvel comics line, as well as STAG, FOR MEN ONLY, ACTION FOR MEN, and MALE. These men's magazines perpetuate Goodman's "symbol syndrome," and display a diamond on the covers, instead of the "red circle."

The Red Circles included, among others, three weird menace titles: MYSTERY TALES (March, 1938 through May, 1940--nine issues); UNCANNY TALES (April, 1938 through May, 1940--five issues--and not to be confused with UNCANNY STORIES, a science fiction publication, or the Canadian UNCANNY TALES); and REAL MYSTERY (April and July, 1940). There was little difference between the three magazines, in fact, too little, in one case, since the first issue of REAL MYSTERY contained mostly reprints (retitled) from the other two. Like Ace, the company didn't stint on house names, such as Caldwell Pierce, Paul Howard (who was Henry Treat Sperry), Taylor Ward (Alan Hyde), John Trask, Alan Blake (Omar Gwinn), and Douglas Giles (James Hall). Robert O. Erisman was editor of these titles. He began his career as a copywriter in advertising, later wrote for both pulps and slicks.

Another trick it picked up, this time from Popular, was the suggestive story heading, aimed at stopping the customer cold (or hot) in his tracks. Glancing through a typical issue, you would have been convinced it was boiling over with lascivious actions, from the likes of "Satan Is My Lover," "Debutantes for the Damned," "Pawn of Hideous Desire," "Hell's Hallowed Housewives," "Blood Is My Bride," "Honeymoon in Hell," "Lovely Daughters of Madness." When reprinting an earlier story, the editor made doubly sure the new title struck the right titillating note. "Dweller in Darkness" became "Four-Handed Fiancee," "Lucifer's Bride" was changed to "I, Satan, Take Thee, Sin Child," and "Listen to the Devil's Drum" appeared later as "Dead Mates for the Devil's Devotees." Story promotion in the Red Circles hit a fever pitch.

**Big Nerve-Crawling Feature-Length Novelette of
Satan's Last Lust-Spawned Lieutenant**

**Spine-Raking Eerie-Terror Novelette of Hollywood's
Hell-Born Handmaidens**

**A Girl Debased, a Girl Who Had Learned the Lure
Of Things Unspeakable**

Phrases used over and over included "Brain Numbing," "Soul Blasting," "Blood Bursting." Indeed, if you absorbed too many of these stimulants too fast, you'd need a tranquilizer before going on to sample the stories themselves.

As for covers, some of the most seductive women yet seen appeared in the Red Circle line. Some were rendered by our old friend, Norman Saunders, one of the best delineators of alluring femininity found in the pulps. But all the females were glorious, as they were subjected to the usual tortures and torments, barely a grimace to mar their classic features. No matter what was happening to them, they struck a provocative pose. The voluptuous redhead enclosed in a glass jar exudes enough fiery passion to melt her way out. The blond, her hair held by a knife-wielding fiend, her body barely covered, just naturally looks erotic in her kneeling position. The auburn-haired creature, chained before a ray machine, stretches her arms in a sensual supplication.

"Lovely Daughters of Madness" in **Mystery Tales,** September, 1939, was typical Graham: fast-moving, plenty of shocks, like these gals getting their kicks, and an abrupt resolution at the end with the villain un-masked.

It seemed that everything Manvis touched turned to lust. Some of its cops-and-robbers pulps, like DETECTIVE SHORT STORIES, flaunted nude gals on the covers, at the mercy of leering fiends, even though the stories had to do with detectives and policemen solving crimes. And MARVEL SCIENCE STORIES, a mediocre science fiction pulp, flirted with eroticism for six issues in its illustrations, but not in the stories, before unaccountably turning on the sex-sadism for two issues; afterwards, it lapsed back into mainstream science fiction.

The stories in the Red Circles suffered the usual pulp aches and pains. Pulp writing was not noted for its complexity, and under no stretch of the imagination, could these be considered as intricate works of art. While the writing was smooth, the emphasis was on shock effect. Here, as elsewhere, the single-event approach was used, with a buildup to one happening after another, but little unified cohesiveness.

There was far less inventory taking in the Red Circles than in the Spicies. But you didn't have to search long to find something mildly stimulating.

- He became intensely aware of her full-blown figure in a tight-fitting, low-cut dress which brought into prominence every curve of her body. Her breasts rose and fell; her lips were half-open with invitation.
- And she must have read my thoughts, for her lips were parted, her beautifully formed young breasts tossed in frenzy, and her eyes pleaded with me hotly.
- Her small round breasts, standing pertly upright, seemed to tremble with her emotion.

Stylistically, the authors kept their deliveries short and

snappy, often, one-syllabic, refreshing after so much earlier atmospheric meanderings in other publications. For instance:

"I undressed, turned out the light, got into bed, but did not lie down. I looked at the table, its top in a pool of moonlight--and for a brief moment I thought I could see again the head of the old man in its middle. Nonsense, of course."

Openings wasted no time getting to the bare facts:

"With a gloating chuckle, the man crouched over the limp, pulsating body of his victim. A low moan of returning consciousness broke from the girl's bleeding lips; a shuddering tremor shook her rounded thighs."

The emphasis was on pain--a pain that merged into a burning craving, as the victim yearned for gratification.

"And yet--with her, dimly, some mysterious force was surging through her arteries, exciting her, disturbing her so that her thighs trembled and a throbbing warmth of desire pulsed through them, causing her hips to undulate upward gently, sinuously. Slowly, even as she hated the thought, she began to enjoy the bite of those ants; she began to long for the caresses of anything which would hurt her, anything which would rise to meet this bewildering passion which surged up inside her. . ."

Unfortunately, it wasn't all good, honest, clean fun. Generally, such hot, surging ardor was brought to this volcanic pitch by such sneaky tricks as administering aphrodisiacs. In some issues, nearly half the stories made use of drugs and narcotics. In the face of such glib explanations, the effect might border on the ridiculous. By way of illustration: the hero enters a temple of pagan love, accompanied by the villain. A young Egyptian girl, with large and limpid eyes, and lovely, unclad body, clings to his side. Other participants posture on deep divans about the room. When the hero kills the nemesis, the spell is broken. He had been hypno-

Saunders again, with an auburn-haired beauty whose charms are circumspectly hidden (as was the case in these situations), while the typical cowled villain and his henchman prepare her for a death worse than fate, in this August, 1939 scene.

tized, his will weakened and subjected to suggestion through the use of drugs. The temple is revealed as a dingy room, his paramour as a middle-aged, haggard creature, and the revelers as simply figments of his imagination. Many stories proceeded along similar lines, although few were as utterly unconvincing, with the principals obsessed, without realizing it, their doom seemingly foreordained, until they suddenly regained their responsible state and found they had been surreptitiously fed drugs.

MYSTERY TALES and UNCANNY TALES (and later, REAL MYSTERY) came on the scene too late to have earned this condemnation by Bruce Henry, although they, probably more than any of the other weird menace publications, might have precipitated it. From the AMERICAN MERCURY (April, 1938):

"This month, as every month, 1,508,000 copies of terror magazines, known to the trade as the shudder group, will be sold throughout the nation. . .They will contain enough illustrated sex perversion to give Kraft-Ebbing the unholy jitters."

Strong words, indeed. The fact is, though, they were more dramatic than definitive. There may have been some truth to them, but much more supposition. Perversion simply was not part of a pulp presentation–another case of a critic jumping to a conclusion undoubtedly based on a cursory glance rather than a comprehensive examination. Maybe the covers decided him. At that time, there was plenty of visual emphasis on torture, certainly. This critical fixation has continued to the present. The weird menace magazines today often are referred to by the generic term, "sex-sadism," as if that was all they ever dealt in. Granted, there was a good amount of that during, roughly, a three-year period. But then, of course, the all-out exploitation of sex-sadism covered only a third of their lifetime. A more appropriate designation would be plain old "horror-terror." Or how about "weird menace?"

So, back to our subject, namely, sex-sadism. Perhaps no author characterized the pulsating, passion-charged approach of the Red Circles better than Donald Graham. He was as much a master plotter (in shorter form) as Norvell Page. There were drawbacks to this breathless pace of his, just as there were to Page's and many others'. He didn't take time to develop a genuine motivation, in many cases, and depended heavily on drugs for his *deus ex machina*. His sadism was blatant. His heroes often were nothing more than manipulated stock characters, hardly anything new, as I said. And yet he could generate such an acrid, pervasive emotionalist, always on the verge of exploding, you almost felt it.

This is demonstrated in his first appearance in print, in
HORROR STORIES (October-November, 1938). "Revolt of
the Circus Freaks" set the stage for later similar themes: the
misfits and malignants shunned by society who take their
revenge by torturing fair maidens. In equating evil with
deformity, he continued a weird-menace assumption: the
more abnormal, misshapen and misanthropic a character, the
more certain the reader could be that he was all bad. Warped
body, warped mind.

"Revolt" has to do with a bacchanal presided over by
abandoned, sadistic freaks who deform their victims, then
place them on display. Various depravities are described,
with the inevitable "villain-who-stands-to-profit" behind the
whole thing. The author's staccato style and vivid expression-
ness make this a terror *tour de force.* It's revolting, but
engrossing.

For the Red Circle magazines Graham unleased similar
fiendishnesses, in half a dozen stories, suitably titled such as:
"Mates for Hell's Half-World Minions," "Scourge of the
Corpse-Clan," "Yield, Lovely Maidens, to the Blood-Master,"
and "Satan Lives for My Love."

In one, the hero, drugged as usual, and unaware of his
condition succumbs to every beautiful body he meets.

". . .she saw the look in my eyes, realizing only dimly the
meaning of what she read there--the salacious caressing of her
body with my eyes, like lewd hands exploring a nakedness,
the bestial, lusting pictures that ran through my imagination,
sending the blood pounding through my veins and thrills of
delight rippling over my body."

Since it was impossible to actually bring off a sexual
encounter in the pulps, Graham niftily got around this taboo
by setting some of the more risque elements in the imagination. With the drug miraculously timed to stop-watch

precision, the hero swoons in a red haze as the apparent sexual crisis arrives, only to awaken later convinced he has killed the girl, whose body is still beside him, after profaning her.

No publication of this type--or any type, for that matter-- went for long without an Arthur Burks story; the Red Circle magazines were no exception. Once again, here's an example of his ability to get by on very little plot. In "The Flesh-Hungry Phantoms," in UNCANNY TALES (March, 1940), the hero investigates fur thefts. He comes upon a group of uninhibited, lewd women. They surround him in the fur loft, nearly smothering him under the garments. He responds to the thrill of the lusting nude bodies and caressing, possessive furs. The women taunt and tempt him at the same time. Willingly, he becomes their pawn and allows them to subjugate his will to theirs. And that's about it--not much more than a series of cloying descriptions. But how often do you find transvestism, fetishism, seduction and sado-masochism all in one pulp story? Now, please under- stand: this bold documentation of deviationism was unusual for the pulps. If straight lovemaking didn't appear, then perversion had no chance at all. Adultery, promiscuity, moral corruption--these ideas got an airing, that's true, but in terms of implication, not explication.

In the Graham selection, what the hero imagines is cleverly interwoven with actual events, to indicate an approaching crisis of mad passion. It's a matter of inference, though nothing happens. The hero never touches the girl, of course; the poor guy passes out first. This "hands-off" policy was widely practiced. Thus, in another instance, two couples come under the influence of a strange man. He uses drugs and hypnotism, as well as a love philtre (unknown to them, of course), to entangle them in an extra-marital relationship,

Once more, we see a similarity in covers, between this one, for the March, 1938 **Dime Mystery**, and the next, for **Thrilling Mystery**. In the case of Popular Publications' mystery-terror magazines, the covers were sometimes distinguished by backgrounds more lurid than foregrounds.

From the September, 1938 issue, the girl in the background can barely be seen. It's interesting to note that despite **Thrilling Mystery's** avowed interest in torture situations, few of the covers and stories explored this theme.

as vengeance on them for the sins of their mothers. The following episode suggests an approaching consummation which, of course, never takes place.

"For there below me in that room my Penelope, my beloved bride of four short months--incredible horror of it!-- was dancing with her cousin, John Carter--stark naked! The wild look of animal lust was in their eyes as they danced. They weaved and undulated in a sinuous Oriental rhythm, approaching each other and retreating. They made no sound --their eyes alone spoke, spoke of desire, of unspeakable things."

I don't know how you can speak of unspeakable things. But anyway, if the authors talked evasively about sexual matters, they didn't hesitate to yell murder and detail mayhem. One of the most lurid of the sex-sadistic accounts is Russell Gray's "Fresh Fiances for the Devil's Daughter," found in MARVEL TALES (May, 1940). It's extremely depraved, and certainly not for the squeamish. A beautiful woman traps the men--and their wives--who spurned her. She sets out to make them suffer. The women are hung by their wrists from the ceiling, and burned with hot irons in various sensitive areas. Each excess on the part of the torturess stirs up her passion to a white heat, and she avidly seeks a lover to cool off her ardor before continuing with further cruelties.

This was an extreme case. Very few stories reached this unedifying level of repugnancy. Some, in fact--not many, it's true--practiced a commendable restraint, with no sexual overtones. Frederick C. Davis' "Nameless Brides of For- bidden City" comes to mind in this respect. The story, in UNCANNY TALES (April-May, 1939) takes place in Lhasa, the mysterious Tibetian city. In adopting such a far-off locale, the author keeps the local color confined to what readily came to hand, like an encyclopedia (since undoubtedly, he had never been there). At least, several passages smack of text-book treatment. These stories generally avoided such exotic settings, sticking to American surroundings. But never let it be said that a pulp author hesitated to conduct his audience where he had never been. If he didn't know anything about the place, they didn't either.

Anyway, that should have been the case. But it wasn't always. One author has mentioned how he, too, set his action in Tibet. Since nobody knew anything about the country, he figured, the editor would accept whatever he wrote. One time at a party he was bragging about his methods. "Some guy I'd never seen before asked how I could write about a place I'd never been. I said I knew the country had mountains and was cold; so all my stories were laid at night, and all that could be seen were the mountains, moon and faces in fine light. About that time somebody introduced me to the man I was talking to, who had just come back from spending considerable time in Tibet. I don't think I ever wrote another story about Tibet."

Similar problems find similar solutions. In his story, Davis confines most of the action to nighttime, too. Very simply, the plot is this: A son is born to an American couple in Lhasa. At the time of his birth, the Grand Lahma breathes his last. According to ancient beliefs, the spirit of Buddha slips from that exalted personage at his death and enters a newborn babe--in this case, the American infant. So it becomes a matter of the couple preventing their son being taken from them, and at the same time, making their escape from the forbidden city.

Other authors seen in the Red Circle magazines included Wayne Rogers, Donald Dale, Wyatt Blassingame, John H. Knox, Henry Kuttner, Ray Cummings, Leon Byrne, Mindret

Lord and Robert Leslie Bellem. Some appeared but once or twice, possibly because of the sexual emphasis in the magazines. This turned off several authors. Paul Ernst, for one, had little to do with it. "When the heat was put on for sadism, I officially bowed out," he said recently.

By the time MYSTERY NOVELS AND SHORT STORIES came out, in 1939, sex-sadism was nearing its end. The magazine capitalized on the trend, though, with luscious females on the covers suffering the usual ignominies: whippings, roastings and mad-virus inoculations. It went through an erratic publishing and pricing schedule, typical of some other Double Action titles put out by Winford. This particular "Blue Ribbon" pulp carried a fifteen-cent price tag to begin with, then went to ten cents, and back up to fifteen cents again. Ostensibly published every other month, it skipped six months between issue number five (December, 1939) and number six (July, 1940), and four months between number six and the final issue (December, 1940).

The history of this publication was one of change. Although it started with volume one, number one, in 1939, it was a derivation of MYSTERY NOVELS, which dated from 1931. At that time, Doubleday Doran was publishing a fat quarterly bearing that title, and selling for a quarter a copy. Each issue contained three complete detective mysteries, of some fifty thousand words each, by such authors as Vincent Starrett, Philip MacDonald, H. Bedford-Jones, John W. Vandercook (later, a radio news analyst), and Leslie Charteris (of "The Saint" fame). The company divested itself of its pulp line in the mid-thirties, to concentrate on book publishing. Louis H. Silberkleit's Winford Company, which got started in 1934, began publishing a magazine called MYSTERY NOVELS, that, he reports, was not a continuation of the other. "We didn't take the Doubleday

On a few occasions, science fiction-type situations were utilized by the weird menace pulps. These two other-worldly no-gooders on this November, 1939 cover may not last long, even if the hero misses; apparently, they forgot their oxygen tanks.

magazine over," Silberkleit said recently. "We used the same title, but they never sued us or anything."

The new version that followed the Doubleday pulp and continued only a short while was slimmed down, with one novel and a few short stories. The emphasis was on weird crime, along the following lines.

"Aboard the transatlantic dirigible, Jupiter, flying high over the storm-tossed ocean, was a cargo of sudden and unexpected death. It took the best deductive powers of Christopher Hand, famous criminologist, to track down the sinister, hooded murderer who climbed the girders and slunk along the catwalks with death following in his wake."

At this time (1937), Winford was publishing some sixteen pulp titles. They listed twenty the following year, and twenty-eight when MYSTERY NOVELS AND SHORT STORIES appeared. By then, the company carried the name, Double Action Magazines, and put "Blue Ribbon" as a distinctive designation, on its covers. MYSTERY NOVELS had been allowed to languish. The new version now presented short stories of various lengths, editorially grouped under headings like "novel," and "novelette," and preceded by such mouth-watering phrases as "Spine-Chilling," "Blood-Curdling," and "Mystery Filled." Cliff Campbell was listed as editor--another name from the pulps' never-ending house name rolls. Actually, Abner J. Sundell, later editorial director of the company, handled this chore.

In the usual tradition, the forgotten genius in charge of titles and story synopses, made sure that each entry connoted an illicit relationship. Here are a few representations: "Courtship of the Vampire," "Hall of Crawling Desire" (with the crawling done by cockroaches), "Bride of the Stone-Age Ripper," "Mate of the Demon," "Murder Lust in 'C'" (that is, lust for a hidden necklace), "Mistress of the Undead," "Satan Takes a Wife," "Mistress of the Murder Madmen," and "Bride of the Ape." A typical tagline went like this:

Tale of Passionless Pain-Lusting Disciples
For Satan's Legion of the Damned!

What the longer blurbs lacked in pithy alliteration, they compensated for in suggestiveness.

"I feared for Evelyn's life in that corpse-town shambles. . . until I found my dear betrothed in a satyr's rendezvous--a wanton bacchante lost in murder-mad revelry!"

The covers proclaimed the following: HORROR-TERROR -WEIRD! Unfortunately, these words had been bandied about so promiscuously by then, they had just about lost all

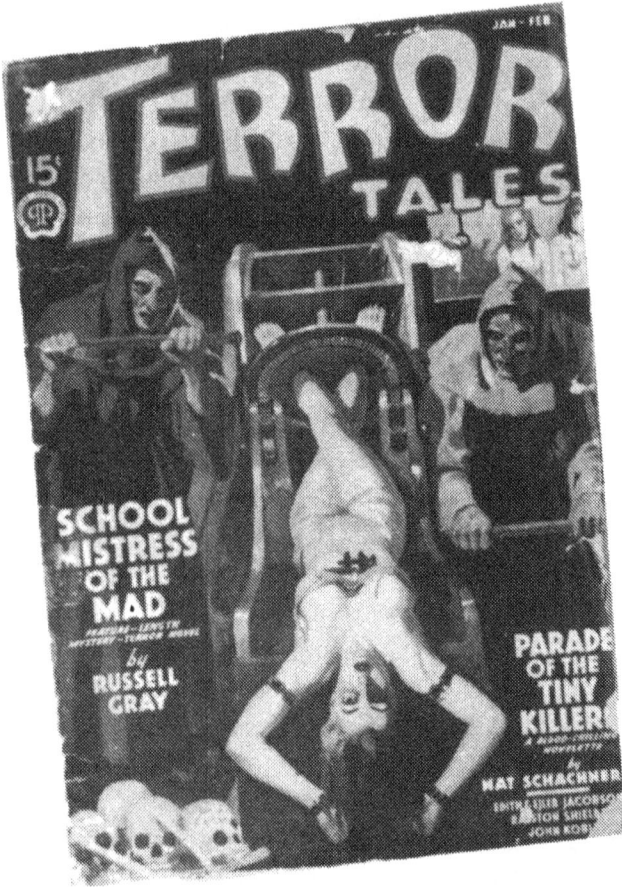

Here may be a torture contrivance to end all pain devices—January-February, 1939.

effect. Some of those elements appeared in the stories, but not much worth noting. Many of the bylines were apparently house names, such as Cliff Campbell, Vernon James, James Rourke, Zachary Strong and Harold Ward. Established writers found in these pages were in the minority. Among the few were Arthur J. Burks, G. T. Fleming-Roberts and Frank Belknap Long, Jr.

It's not necessary to summarize any of the stories. However, a few of the ideas might be touched on. In "The Beasts That Terror Spawned," by Lazar Levi (December, 1939), a degenerate band operates a torture ship, where young girls are prepared to be sold into slavery. Despite the sadistic overtones, lurid descriptions were kept to a minimum –quite different from the policy in the Red Circle magazines, of course. This story, incidentally, may have set some sort of record in weird-menace literature for unmasking the villain by the ninth page, with ten still to go. The main aim of the authors seemed to be to make the murders as gory as possible. When a killer searches for diamonds hidden in an apartment, he finds it necessary, for some reason, to practically slash his victims' heads from their bodies. Elsewhere, the evil nemesis uses a distillate of South American plants to drive birds into a frenzy, with the result that they bloodily peck their victims to death.

The Double Action line also included REAL NORTH WEST ADVENTURES, 5 STAR WESTERN, SUPER SPORTS, BLUE RIBBON WESTERN and DOUBLE ACTION DETECTIVE, among others. Like the Red Circle magazines, there was some spillover of weird menace into

This May-June, 1938 cover has another cringing victim about to be branded—a favorite pastime in these mysterious sanctums—while some poor soul is being rudely buffeted about elsewhere.

other publications. At one point, the company advertised a forthcoming BLUE RIBBON HORROR, but it was never published. Some of the stories planned for that issue (if any were, that is) may have ended up elsewhere, maybe in something like the January 1939 DOUBLE-ACTION DETECTIVE, with its weird menace cover and partial weird contents.

The company paid a half cent a word, either through arrangement, or on publication. Naturally, this policy worked to the advantage of the publisher, rather than the author, who might wait months and months for publication, so he could be paid, only to find his manuscript turned down after all, or the company out of business. Payment on publication generally characterized a none-too-solvent operation. But the Winford Company kept going. In the forties, the company expanded its comic book line (such as THE SHIELD and THE WIZARD), as did so many other pulp publishers.

Years before, Silberkleit had worked for Hugo Gernsback, the father of science fiction. A struggling publisher in the late thirties, Silberkleit became a rich man through the Archie Comics group, according to Robert A. W. Lowndes. (And he still heads the Archie company.) Lowndes worked for him for twenty years, editing the Columbia line of science fiction magazines, known as the Double Action group. As he says of Silberkleit in the PULP ERA (May-June, 1967): "He had a natural charm and warmth about him, which turned out to be genuine, even though more earthy qualities showed up when a very volatile temper displayed itself. You knew where you stood with him; if he was displeased, he didn't hesitate to say so, and when displeased, his voice could carry to the elevators."

CHAPTER XI. THE DEFECTIVE DETECTIVES

We defy you to produce another hero-detective in the entire realm of mystery fiction so unusual.
Editorial
STRANGE DETECTIVE MYSTERIES
(October, 1937)

The pulps suffered a notorious failing. Ironically, the crafty, scheming villains often were more interesting than the stoic, incorruptible heroes. You might not relate to the bad guys, but you enjoyed their fits of temper, their unprincipled passions, their involved conspiracies and their obsessive dementia. After all, it was just good, dirty fun.

So what would happen if the heroes were "humanized" by taking on a few of these characteristics? What indeed? It happened. The event took place in DIME MYSTERY--five years to the month since the magazine switched from detective to weird menace. This time, the emphasis was on weird crime fighters, flawed do-gooders, so to speak, investigators with an affliction or deformity that hampered their activities. They made their debut in the October 1938 issue, amid editorial ballyhoo proclaiming the great occasion.

Sometime earlier, the editor had noted that the magazine was doing what everyone had said was impossible: namely, providing entire issues "concerned with weird, fantastic

151

subjects placed in eerie, terror-inspiring surroundings." This time he pointed out once more how the sceptics were prophesying failure on the latest change. He hailed the new type of story as something "brand new in the entire field of magazine fiction," overflowing with "all the eerie menace and weirdly terrifying atmosphere, plus speed, dramatic punch, plot complication and breathless tempo of the best detective mysteries." Perhaps the idea was to promise the reader so much, so fast, he would forget just what he was supposed to get, and thus couldn't hold anyone accountable. Continuing in the same modest vein, the announcement guaranteed "the sort of robust, vigorous, thrill-packed melodrama that could hold any reader on the edge of his chair right to the last line, feeling that he actually knew the characters were flesh and blood like himself, and that everything they did was honestly and humanly and logically motivated." Since no writer, pulp or slick, could live up to that standard of perfection, none tried.

They fulfilled one commitment, though, by creating "weird, fantastic subjects." Nothing could be much more incredible in the way of a crime fighter than the types taking over the magazine at this time. It was a bid for reader sympathy--clumsy and contrived, but also, appealing, in a desultory sort of way.

Take John Kobler's character, Peter Quest. Here was a private eye who couldn't see. In each story, he suffered a recurrent attack of glaucoma, which temporarily blinded him just at the crucial moment, naturally. Then he would recover, never the worse for wear. He was the first of many eccentrically handicapped individuals who fought crime during the next two years in the magazine. In that time, the main characters suffered enough infirmities to keep a team of diagnosticians busy a lifetime.

The first issue, October, 1937, of **Strange Detective Mysteries** introduced several odd detective heroes—precursors of the "defective detectives" **Dime Mystery** featured.

There was a pronounced leanness and pallor about Nat Perry. No, it wasn't due to an artistic temperament. He was a hemophiliac, you understand, nicknamed The Bleeder. Regularly, he ducked bullets, knives and assorted lethal attacks, when the slightest scratch would cause his death. The writing team of Edith and Ejler Jacobson enjoyed thrusting him into impossible situations, and having him escape by the skin of his skin. Ejler Jacobson was to spend the next fourteen years with Popular Publications, in editorial duties. Today, he serves as the science fiction editor of GALAXY and IF. Only now, he spells his last name, Jakobsson.

In the thirties, he adopted a simplified spelling. "We had so much trouble with my name," he relates, "that I was going through life having to spell it. But it really got to me once, at the public library. The girl filling out my card asked me my name. I said E-J-L-E-R. She asked, 'How do you spell that?' " Jakobsson came to this country from Finland in 1926. He earned a bachelor's degree at Columbia in 1935, when he met his wife-to-be, who also earned a B.A. degree that year, at Barnard College. That same year he started writing for the pulps.

Leon Byrne's character, Dan Holden, another impaired

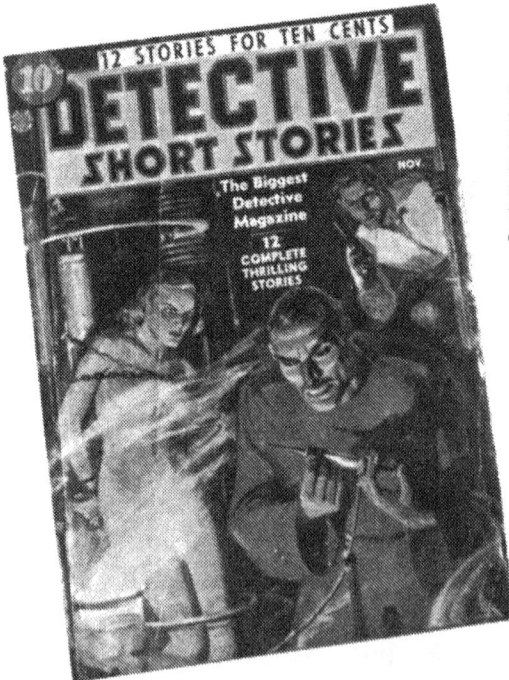

Detective Short Stories—this is the second issue, November, 1937, with a cover by J.W. Scott—emphasized horror-terror in the illustrations, although the stories featured detective heroes.

Sadism was not as obvious on the **Detective Short Stories** covers (this one is dated April, 1938) as on the Red Circle mystery-terror issues.

hero, had had his hearing destroyed by a gunman's bullet. He wore a silver plate in his head and was so adept at lip reading, even his secretary didn't know he was deaf. Nat Schachner's character, Nicholas Street, was an amnesiac, so named for the street where he was found. His crime-fighting career took the form of a fruitless search for his past.

The stories followed the gory direction of earlier material. Murder was always gruesome. "Weltering in a corner was a thing blackened and charred and heaving wetly like hot tar." One guess what that had been. On another occasion, a victim is enveloped by green tentacular fronds growing out of his body, until he was "no longer recognizable as a man, but just a bloated tangled mass of slimy vegetation."

Just in case the readers didn't take to this new hero-image, the editor gave them various pep talks from time to time. Soon after the change, he was enthusing how the magazine now combined the "principal elements of the old with the freshness and novelty of the new." Later, he commented: "But murder is not the only fine art connected with the subject of death. The detection of murder is also an art--

and a very fine one indeed. . .It is this pursuit, this conflict of two fine arts in the great drama of death that--we feel-- provides the greatest reading thrills of all time." Obviously, someone was proud of something. No telling what, though, since there was little detection, even less artistry.

The "defective detective" period was a barren interlude. At first, violence took on epidemic proportions. Then a seda- tive was administered, toning the stories down. Finally, the fever burnt itself out, as the contents almost turned common- place. By the end of 1940, DIME MYSTERY made a half- hearted and brief return to weird menacism, before shelving the horror for good. Before the end, the crime-stoppers had become almost prosaic, often with nothing more than an unusual name or blighted background as credentials. Some latecomers: Loring Dowst's character, Pendexter Riddle, the "extraordinary question mark;" Dale Clark's Ghostly Jones, the poltergeist specialist; Dane Gregory's Rocky Rhodes and Satan Jones; Ralph Oppenheim's Daniel Craig, the Bystander; Stewart Sterling's Jim Big-Knife, last of the Kwanee Black- feet and Wyatt Blassingame's Joe Gee, the detective who couldn't sleep while on a case. As new criminologists were introduced, the old motivational gimmicks were kicked out. The ultimate in non-incentiveness must have been Willard D'Arcy's John R. Parkhill, who became a private detective "because it annoyed the police." The critics were right after all; it couldn't be done.

The attempt to provide "thrill-packed melodrama" wasn't a total failure, though. A few of the private eyes proved interesting; one of the most successful was a creation of Russell Gray's. He had tried to put across a character called Calvin Kane, who was saddled with a deformed body, and siddled like a crab as he dragged his withered right leg along. One shoulder was six inches higher than the other. But he

Dane Gregory, brother of Wayne Robbins (Ormond Gregory), contributed Rocky Rhodes (the name, I guess, implying the tough time he was having as an escaped convict turned private eye) to the lineup of "defective detectives" in **Dime Mystery**. "Scalps for the Butcher" is from the March, 1940 issue.

had one physical advantage: arms like steel. He was simply too grotesque to last. However, his endowment became the touchstone for the fame of Ben Bryn. Suffering from infantile paralysis as a child, Bryn was forced to push himself around on a wheeled platform. This put "tremendous power into his arms and iron in his soul." When he gained the use of his withered legs, "through sheer grit by heartbreaking exercises," he became a sort of fore-shortened Paul Bunyan, five feet tall and prodigiously strong. The saga of Ben Bryn continued in DIME MYSTERY for several years, through various format changes, and helped Gray make the switch to detective writing that led to his later success in hard covers.

The inspiration (well then, progenitor, if you will) for the defective detectives came from Popular's STRANGE DETECTIVE MYSTERIES. This magazine came out in 1937, at ten cents a copy. The first issue (October) carried this introduction:

"Remember the time you read that one perfect knockout detective story--bizarre, mysterious, thrill-packed, different? . . .We give you. . .not only one bizarre, thrilling, eerie-laden mystery story such as you've searched for, but a whole magazine full of them!. . .Here is detective mystery, strange, extraordinary--bizarre!"

Which just goes to show that the authors hadn't cornered all the lamentable adjectives. The question is, why wasn't it titled BIZARRE DETECTIVE MYSTERIES?

Norvell Page led off the issue, sporting the title: "America's No. 1 Master of the Extraordinary Mystery Tale." His hero, Dunne, was an expert at ju-jitsu, which of course, stood him in good stead. He had unusual quarters, rigged with chairs that slid forward by themselves, and a talking cigar box--guaranteed to disconcert the visitor. In the same issue, Paul Ernst's Seekay sallied forth, his face masked so no one could see it. Then there was Arthur Leo Zagat's kindly Dr. John Bain, always ready to help the poor, and obviously derived from the author's Doc Turner series in THE SPIDER MAGAZINE.

Other unusual crime fighters appeared in subsequent issues. They ranged from policemen to secret heroes, such as Donald G. Cormack's Schuyler Montgomery, an attorney, known to the underworld both as Dr. Hand and the Parson, and Gray's super detective, Ethan Burr (with the Fischer byline). Wyatt Blassingame's Bill Long, the Thin Man, performed in a circus for a living and solved crimes for fun, with the help of sideshow freaks.

The magazine, too, emphasized revolting murders. "Keeney looked down at the shapeless mass of flesh which jellied loosely over the stretcher. The eyes looked like marbles which had been dropped into the mud puddle of the man's featureless countenance." Promotion-wise, the magazine bore an affinity with the weird menace pulps.

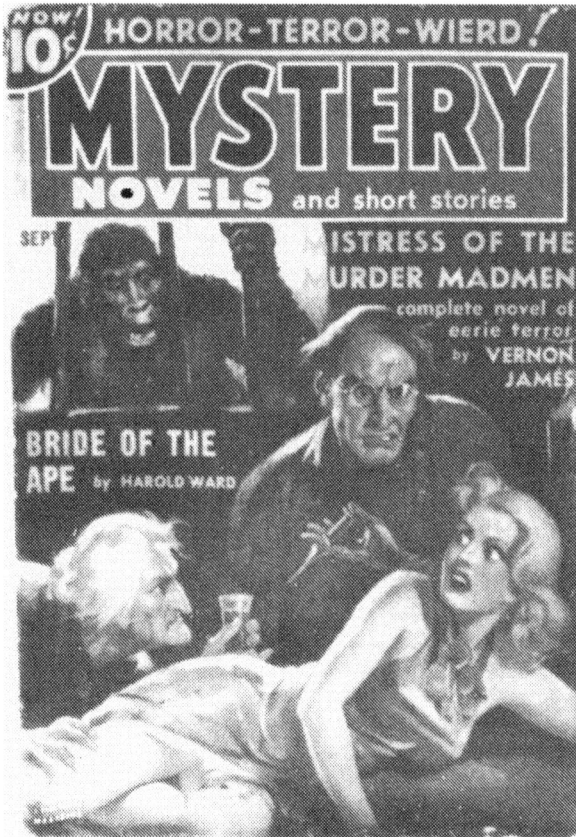

This September, 1939 issue follows the cover tradition then popular, but the stories do not live up to this advance publicity. Some of the heroes here are detective types. A misspelled word on the cover—in this case, Weird—was a rarity, and in fact, most pulps had very few typographic errors.

"No barred door could stop the fiendish, corpse-defiling thing that prowled Park Avenue on its hideous trail of slaughter! No bullet could turn it from its trackless course! High in the luxurious, sacrosanct tower apartments of New York's Four Hundred it struck again--and vanished. . .Would Eagle Coyle, the ace detective, dare follow a hunch to the invisible killer's inviolate murder chambers--when the lovely girl over whom he stood sleepless vigil was next on its grisly list?"

You know by now, of course, that all this concern over the creature's invulnerability was just so much editorial propaganda. In STRANGE DETECTIVE MYSTERIES, particularly, it turned out that the fiend used tricks to overpower his victims, just as the blurb writer did here. The magazine differed from the typical mystery-terror pulp in that the emphasis was usually on weird crime, rather than weird menace. And the heroes were lawmen and the like, instead of average citizens, which, perhaps, took away any lingering doubt as to the outcome. In any case, the combination was successful. Edited by Willard Crosby, Ejler Jacobson and John Bender at different times, STRANGE DETECTIVE MYSTERIES enjoyed a long run, lasting into the war.

CHAPTER XII. FEMMES FATALES

She was gorgeous. She was an exotic passion-flower, a scarlet voluptuary of the mysterious East, a beautiful serpent in whose fathomless eyes all the sins and lusts of the world seemed to have congregated.

"Mistress of the Murder Madmen"
MYSTERY NOVELS AND SHORT STORIES
(September, 1939)

Of all the themes in mystery-terror fiction, one of the most provocative is the alluring temptress weaving a seductive spell to ensnare the hero in her wicked schemes. The weird menace approach is more greatly heightened by the modern Circe, say, than the detective story by a hardboiled murderess, or the western by a tobacco-chewing female trail boss. Femmes fatales appeared frequently as menace-figures. Although they are now no more remembered than the incorruptible heroes they worked their wiles on, many were interesting women of mystery. Often, you wished that they had stayed around longer. It seemed a shame to throw all that good glamour away quickly.

In these stories, the seductress vamped the principal (or threatened him in some way) because (1) she wanted him for herself (usually, because of his money); (2) she plotted revenge; (3) she wanted something he had, but didn't want him. Often, she operated with a confederate, who also stood to gain, and who, of course, remained completely unsuspected until the end.

The situation was complicated, in most cases, by the fact that the hero's wife or sweetheart came under direct danger. Temporarily under the control of the seductress (as for instance, because of drugs), the hero might actually threaten his own wife.

"The most sinisterly beautiful woman in the world stood beside me, bidding me plunge the dagger I held into the nude body of the lovely girl on the altar before us--my wife! Terror seized me in its icy grip, and every decent instinct in me shrieked in protest. Yet I raised the deadly knife. . ."

There are many examples of each of the three categories. The idea of the temptress after the hero and his money was used by THRILLING MYSTERY, where stories involving sinister women appeared infrequently. "Blood of Witches," by Paul Ernst (October, 1935) describes an exotic seer with a "darkly beautiful face with great black eyes and lips as red as blood." She is a crystal gazer, who warns of witch blood in the hero's fiancee. The crystal shows the couple an evil manifestation of the girl, a menacing, vulpine creature. Later, both she and the hero seem to take on the characteristics of wolves. The plot was to drive the hero to murder his fiancee, so the mystic could have him--and his wealth--for herself.

A similar entrapment develops in "Open the Dead Door," by Alexander Faust, in UNCANNY TALES (August, 1939). This time, supernaturalism is real, not pretended. The hero meets his wife's sister, whom he hadn't seen since his marriage. She makes it obvious she wants him back for her lover. She holds a party for the couple and other friends, and performs a strange rite. The husband is told to stab a white bird. Reluctantly, he does, as the sister watches.

"She was smiling at me. Not a smile to go with that mad laughter of a moment past, but a slow and tender smile, and sweet--as Rhoda's; and her eyes had grown wider and more brilliantly blue--like Rhoda's--and like--the dead bird's!"

He looks for his wife; she's nowhere to be found. Realizing what has happened, he plunges the knife into the sorceress. If you like morals (and this literature abounds with them), you might say it's dangerous to have too changeable a personality.

. Now for the second motif: revenge. A good example comes from a fast-rising author in 1936, Richard B. Sale. At that time, he was twenty-three, had dropped out of college to write for the pulps, and was already collecting book credits. Within a few years, he would be among the more prolific authors, with several series in detective magazines and bylines in the leading pulps. A book of his on the stands today is "The Oscar."

Usually, the cover girls were depicted as soft, almost languid, in the face of the most fearsome fates. This one, on the June, 1938 **Dime Mystery**, is unusual for the straining, tense pose she strikes as she nears the boiling acid.

His "Rescued by Satan" appeared in MYSTERY AD-VENTURES (May, 1936). A ship in the Mediterranean has been taken over by a beautiful Russian danseuse, her pet, a tiger named Kasha, a fat little captain in her employ, and a tall, thin Russian aristocrat, her suitor. Prisoners on board are a husband and wife, the ship's owner, and his friend, an Egyptologist. The owner explains that the woman is a twin, from the Egyptian town of Bubastis. She was born during the Sothic Month, fulfilling an old superstition that she would be dominated by the cat influence. For eleven months she is normal; on the twelfth, she becomes a human tiger, insane with a fierce urge to kill. Through an early involvement with the ship's owner and his friend, she plans to revenge herself on them. When the Egyptologist is killed, she confides to her lover: " 'After all . . . it is not really murder, Dmitrov. It is only--accident. We do not kill. It is Kasha who kills and Kasha is a dumb beast'--her tones were sardonic--'who has no soul at all . . .' " Later the captain blurts out, " 'The tiger did not kill Reri! She killed him--and blamed it on the tiger . . . With her jaws, her pretty jaws, and her perfect teeth and her lust for blood, she tears out his jugular just as she will tear yours and mine--' "

In this case, the femme fatale takes on the attributes of a wild beast, avid to glut her ferocity on anyone in her way. In Wyatt Blassingame's "The Goddess of Crawling Horrors," in HORROR STORIES (March, 1937), the revenge element is more subtle, but equally deadly. The beguiler is a deathless creature, bent on destroying the grandson of the man who wronged her. When the hero meets her, he is attracted to her colorless, yet ghastly, beauty. "Being near to her was like breathing the heavy fumes of liquor, making him dizzy with passion." She tells him that his father knew her, and his father in turn, and that he shall know her as Death.

Heterosexual deprada-
tions were a common-
place; once in a great
while, an evil temptress
turns against her own
sex, in this Graves
Gladney tableau for
April, 1938.

"She raised a left hand, and for the first time he saw the thing upon the back of it. A great hideous worm rested there, and its head was buried in her flesh! It was eating into her body as into a corpse!

" 'There is no need to fear this worm,' the girl said. 'It is the common end of all of us. They feed on us, and our flesh changes into theirs. But it is not painful. The pain lies in a different kind of worm and a different kind of death.' "

She intends to drive him to kill his sweetheart. As she boasts, " '. . . after tonight my revenge will be full. There will be only one thing left to you: your love for Helen Kay. I leave that so you may see your own actions through her eyes and suffer more horribly.' "

LITTLE MISS DRACULA

by
RALSTON SHIELDS

Ralston Shields, a slick "pulpster" of the period, devised an ingenious vampire story in "Little Miss Dracula," in **Dime Mystery**, August, 1938. Count Nigel Becker-Hazi, it seems, kept his rich and frivolous wife contented with his simulated vampirish love making, only to succumb to a lovely and responsive femme fatale—a real vampire.

Let's now look at an author who was one of the more unusual practitioners of pulp writing, Ralston Shields. He was extraordinary, not for his themes, but for his urbane style and evocative settings. A sultriness suffuses his works, even when concerned with such seamy situations as the following: a jungle doctor who claims supernatural powers to cure a man's wife of a strange desire to kill herself, when all along he intends to barter her to a group of degenerates; and a girl who takes bloody vengeance on a dictator who had mutilated her brother.

Although Shields' output was small--and confined to Popular Publications--it was notable for its subtle handling. He once affirmed that places affected him. "My chief pleasure in life is to go off to some lonely region, and spend days wandering about, absorbing local color, observing the lives of the few people I run across, and above all trying to expose myself to that intangible yet extremely potent quality known as atmosphere." Obviously, a good amount did rub off, for it shows in his stories.

Pulp authors shared one obsession: to get a series of some sort going, so subsequent sales would be more or less a matter of course. This was not too difficult in a detective or science fiction framework, but seldom accomplished in the mystery milieu, which lacked the investigative or inventive hero. However, Shields might be said to have developed a mini-series--several stories with similar treatment and theme, having to do with the temptress who, through apparently occult means, holds the fate of the hero and heroine in her hands. Through an ingratiating style, the opposite of the frenzied pace of someone like Donald Graham, for instance, he brought to his exotic scenes alluring but deadly females and susceptible heroes. He displayed a rich sensuality, a romanticism, if you will.

In "Daughter of the Devil" in HORROR STORIES (October-November, 1937), a couple move into a sea-cliff house with a cathedral-size organ. Playing it one night, the man discovers a mysterious stop. It operates a hidden chamber, that revolves. Within is the femme fatale, a woman whom the hero had once loved. She pretends to have arisen from the dead. Gaining a hold over him, she demands that he place leeches on his sleeping wife's breasts, so she can regain full life by drinking the blood. It is a plot, of course, motivated by revenge, the idea being to induce the husband to murder his wife. Shields projected a variety of moods. Here, a reflective note creeps in, heightened by a touch of piquancy.

"The sound that came from the organ as I played was something quite indescribable. It had the quality of a soft wind rustling on a quiet marsh; it had the quality of muted violins; it had the quality of a woman's voice, a siren's voice, tender and beguiling. And it had something beyond all these: a lazy magic that was almost more like a perfume than a sound."

A similar compelling betrayal takes place on a pleasure cruise, in "Priestess of Pestilence" in TERROR TALES (May-June, 1939). The couple rescue a beautiful Spanish girl off the coast of Mexico. The hero is fascinated by her at the same time he's repelled by a glassy-eyed, hissing chameleon nestled against her breast--an implied witch's familiar, without doubt. She subverts him through seemingly magical means that cause a wasting-away blood fever in his wife. To save her, he must submit to the temptress' desires. Here is the money-motivation situation (the third type), with the enticing beauty and an unsuspected partner (in this case, the wife's uncle, a doctor), attempting to unhinge the wife's mind and to kill the husband for his money.

A high point in this Circe series is seen in "Food for the Fungus Lady" in HORROR STORIES (December-January, 1939-40). There is very little difference in plot between this and the "dead" mistress and her leeches, except that it is richer in atmosphere and even more sophisticated. Again, a couple move into a house, this one once owned by a charlatan astrologer, whom the hero killed for good reason. Pervading the place is a scent of musky perfume, and the thin sound of music, so tenuous as to be almost an imaginary sense-impression. The music leads the husband to the dis-covery of a spring-controlled wall panel. At the end of a hidden passage he comes upon a boudoir-like room, where a lovely woman lies unconscious on a lounge, as a phonograph hypnotically breathes in her ear.

He awakens her to learn that she has lived a hundred years. Naturally, he succumbs to her charms; they enter into an illicit affair. To remain young and vital, she tells him, she must have a fungus, which has to be cultivated from spores placed on his sleeping wife's breast. The temptress is later revealed as the widow of the astrologer, carrying out an involved revenge, to make the husband think his wife suffers a serious malady, so he will kill her.

In his portrayals of male enslavement and female domination--with no breath of sexual abnormality, you understand--Shields pushed the pulp story well beyond its self-confining boundaries. Unfortunately, few other authors were able to follow his lead.

CHAPTER XIII. VARIATIONS ON A THEME

The differences between slick and pulp fiction are by no means as marked as they once were, except in the extremities of both classes. . .Much of the fiction published in the bigger slick magazines these days is pretty close to that in the pulps. And it is because a good story is always a good story, whether pulp or slick.

Frederick Clayton
NEW YORK TIMES (September 7, 1935)

If publishers copied competitors' titles, why couldn't authors copy their own themes? Well, several did, in the weird menace line. In some cases, it was just an idea that was repeated. In others, not only was one topic similar to another, but the entire treatment was duplicated, from the opening, through the development, to the resolution. Deplorable as this practice seems from a creative standpoint, it wasn't objectionable, artistically speaking. It is interesting to see what an author could do with a particular concept, how he varied it, what techniques he employed. Also, repetition often resulted in a more polished presentation, the second or third time around, as happened with Ralston Shields.

Following are examples of four recurring themes. They have been selected as much for their deft presentation, as for the persistency they exemplified. While it's pleasant to cite exemplary accomplishments to keep aesthetic considerations in mind, don't forget, as far as the author was concerned, the whole idea at the beginning was simply to save time and effort. First, a listing of the authors and their general subjects.

1. **W. Wayne Robbins--Man Obsessed.**
2. **Mindret Lord--Woman Without Volition.**
3. **Ray Cummings--Girl Obsessed.**
4. **Donald Dale--Inescapable Doom.**

In contrast to Shields' intoxicating pervasiveness, Robbins excelled in explosive chaos. He was born in 1914 in Pawnee, Oklahoma. He first appeared in print in the July 1939 issue of DIME MYSTERY. "Horror's Holiday Special" was a bravura effort. The protagonist is flung into a jolting nightmare aboard a train. The young man telling the story gives every evidence of derangement. He watches as a girl prepares to eat her dinner. As the waiter lifts the cover of the dish, a gore-spattered head rolls around on the plate. The girl screams, while the man chuckles knowingly. Later, he finds two hands in his suitcase, apparently put there by him. As the mutilations mount, it's obvious a homicidal maniac is running loose, with the hero the logical suspect.

Another situation finds a young man committed to a clinic for care and treatment. His guardians had found him skinning a cat, and feared for his sanity. The doctor insidiously encourages his unhealthy proclivities. After bringing a girl to his room, he loses control of himself, a blackness descends, and he attacks her. The doctor pretends to cover up for him. As the hero rationalizes: "I had found a strange, thrilling new life, one that even big men like Dr. Wilder seemed not to disapprove of." When maimed corpses later are found, he becomes the logical suspect. The hero's fatalistic acceptance of these dilemmas makes his guilt seem all the more certain.

In "Mistress of the Dead," HORROR STORIES (December, 1940), the hero again matter-of-factly accepts his seeming paranoic delusions. As he explains to his relatives: " 'There was a dead woman in my room last night.' " Once again, here's another screwball, who shouldn't be left alone with himself, much less anyone else. Death, a beautiful woman, lures him away from his sweetheart. Of course, the whole thing is a scheme, just as in the other examples. Usually, it's a relative who's trying to give the hero a nervous breakdown or worse. In this case, a cousin covets the young man's money, and uses an accomplice, tricked out in an odd hairdress, with a knife apparently thrust into her heart. However, even with the unmasking, the hero harbors a nagging doubt about his own mental stability.

"I talked collectedly, and they seemed ready enough to

Although flogging as a form of torture was used often by authors, cover artists depended very little on this practice. This is the September-October, 1938 issue.

believe this different person I had become. I wonder if any of those precious psychiatrists ever conceived the fantastic theory that perhaps madness is itself an anti-toxin for madness?--that a person, driven near the limits of mortal endurance, may return cleansed of mind. . .if he returns at all."

Robbins, who did not write under his actual name, which was Ormond Gregory, had a brother, Dane Gregory, who also contributed to these magazines at this time.

Among pulp authors, Mindret Lord holds the distinction of being one of the most polished writers in the field. His copy oozed urbanity. His stories were brief but biting. And his output was surprisingly limited for an author who appeared in Popular's pulps, the Red Circle Magazines, and WEIRD TALES over an eight-year period or so. "Give Me Your Soul," in DIME MYSTERY (April, 1934) has to do with a doctor and a strangely withdrawn young woman he meets. They fall in the clutches of the villain, who is conducting weird experiments. In fact, his researches are downright incredible. It seems he's found out how to force the soul out of a person's body. The girl had escaped from him before he had completed the process, and still had part of her soul left. He explains, " 'Day after day I drive out their souls with pain, renewed and intensified, until that thinking soul abandons all hope of reinhabiting the body it has deserted.' " He puts the couple in a glass bell, under terrific pressure, to perform his treatment. Plaintively, the hero at the end asks for someone to offer them his soul-imbued blood.

It is ludicrous, but probably not more so than many other stories. You must remember that authors frequently didn't take the time to close up the loopholes, when they could spend it more profitably on an outrageous idea for another story.

"Satan Takes a Bride" in HORROR STORIES (August-September, 1936) asks this question "Can you lift from my soul the horror that is making my life an endless hell? Can you prove to me that the woman I am living with is actually the girl I married?"

The evildoer has a yen for the hero's wife. He's found a way to transfer the persona, to divest the material body of its individual dynamicism. " 'I'm going to transfer your wife's personality--soul--will--whatever you call it, to one of these fish. Which shall it be? That slimy eel? The sting ray? No, I think the octopus would make you a better wife. Think of being embraced by eight sucking arms and nibbled, perhaps, by that huge beak!' " He carries out his threat. The man falls into the tank and sure enough, the octopus comes over to nuzzle him. Later, the couple escape. But the man's wife remains peculiarly apathetic. " 'My wife is nothing more than an animated body. She has neither mind, memory, nor interest,' " he is left to bemoan.

To give one further example, here is "Beauty Born in Hell," from HORROR STORIES (August-September, 1939). The Doctor, as he is called, performs "beauty treatments" on his female victims, literally beating them into physical perfection.

" 'You see, it makes very little difference to me whether I get good raw material to start with. Let them be fat or thin-- as ugly as you please--I'll turn out beauties in the end--and as alike as two peas in a pod . . .' "

His "beauty operators" use reducing cabinets, rubber paddles, corrective surgery, electric pins and other pain-inducing devices to break the girls' wills at the same time they are molding their bodies. When remodeled, the look-alikes are presented to the public in a precision dance routine. A concomitant of the purgatorizing process is the

In "Beauty Born in Hell," in **Horror Stories,** August-September, 1939, Mindret Lord shows that beauty is more than skin deep, as his "Doctor" perfects a precision dance routine through a painful process.

complete breakdown of the victim's volition. A reporter's wife becomes one of the Doctor's subjects. In a terse ending, the reporter is left to meditate despairingly: "Physically, she's as perfect as any woman alive; but mentally? She'll do anything she's told, without question or argument– anything. . ."

In contrast to Lord, Ray Cummings was a whirlwind of weird-story creativity in the thirties. He hadn't even hit fifty years of age when he started spewing out a torrent of horror material. But it seemed he had been around for ages, due to the vast amount of space-opera fiction he had written during the twenties.

As a young man, Cummings had served for a while as secretary to Thomas A. Edison. It wasn't long before he took up fiction writing. Today, he is mainly remembered for the science fiction adventures he wrote for the Munsey pulps. ARGOSY's editor at the time, Bob Davis, called him a "Jules Verne returned and an H. G. Wells going forward." Cummings was sixty-nine when he died in 1957.

Detractors have called the Cummings of the thirties a hack, charging that his literary talents had deserted him in his declining years. This was not true. Cummings had been making a good word rate earlier; he fell on leaner days in the thirties, even though by then he was well off financially. So he probably could have taken it easy, if he had wanted. Instead, he (and his wife) turned out a large amount of mystery material. But for all their purposely shocking stagings, his weird stories sometimes showed a fuller grasp of

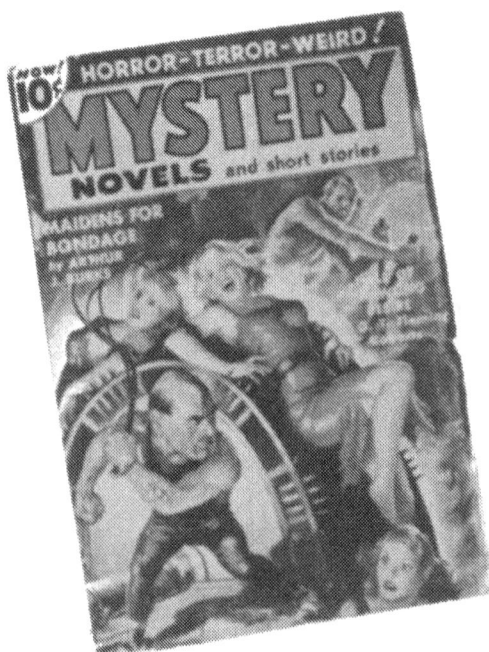

The dwarf, or someone else afflicted in some way, was a favorite villain-type, here seen on the December, 1939 issue of **Mystery Novels and Short Stories,** with no misspellings, this time.

human emotions than much of his reputation-making science fiction. As was true of any pulp writer then, who appeared in four or five magazines each month, Cummings had his share of losers. Many of his finished products needed refinishing. But many others were as good as, or better than, what others were producing.

Cummings paid a lot of attention to the idea of a "girl obsessed." Like Arthur Leo Zagat, he adopted the female viewpoint. Unlike Zagat, and Robbins and his "man-obsessed" representations, Cummings added a prurient flavor to his renditions. His heroines must have been the youngest and at the same time most passionately endowed, of any to grace the pulps. They were sixteen, rarely over seventeen. Yet they exhibited the maturity of women much older. Unfortunately, this bursting young womanhood always seemed to be tainted.

Take the case of Manya Corot, who tells her story in "Death Lives in My Lips," in TERROR TALES (March-April, 1939). "I realize now that we had never been like other families; some intangible foreboding seemed always to be hanging over us." When she falls in love, she finds that her kisses somehow cause the deaths of her lovers. This convinces her she is cursed.

Or what about seventeen-year-old Landa Maine? "I think I was about six years old when I realized that there was something about me that was different from other little girls. . .I think that all my life I knew that I was abnormal." Like Manya, she becomes an unwitting instrument of death. When excited, she scratches--with a pent-up, uncontrollable ardor-- and her scratch is lethal.

Several other fair young things suffered similar delusions. The bedeviled girl in "Wings of Horror," in THRILLING MYSTERY (November, 1937) asks, "Was I indeed what they

"Mistress of the Dead," by Wayne
Robbins, appeared in **Horror Stories** for December, 1940, continuing the author's explosive studies
in obsession—in which the hero is
apparently a deranged killer, but
is actually a victim of a plot.

called a nervous case?. . .Who can separate the real from the
fancied in the thoughts of a young girl? Certainly to me,
everything was real. . .There is nothing more terrifying than
the fear that one's mind is not normal."

For seventeen-year-old Zeta, the wind itself is a monster,
after her. "It was fumbling, hesitant, as though searching,
pausing, bent upon some weird errand. . .There was an eerie
skulkiness to this wind. And then it seemed to find its
objective. . .Then, like a cat jumping a rat, it pounced."

Added to these mental aberrations were the physical depredations inflicted on these heroines. It was always about the same time–that is, just as they were comfortably snuggled in bed--that a panting, lecherous villain in disguise would rudely awaken them.

Thus, Zeta finds someone in her room–a greenish, ghost-like creature who must be the wind monster come to carry her off to its lair. Martha Lane discovers a hooded man in her room, in "Betrothal of the Thing," in MYSTERY TALES (May, 1940). As to be expected, propinquity in the Red Circle magazines always turned to lustful passion.

"She saw the leering, triumphant face come closer, his evil, sensuous eyes glowing strangely. His long fingers drew the bedclothes back slowly, deliberately, until part of her quivering body was exposed to his lewd gaze. . .With the touch of his hands, an incomprehensible submission seemed to come over her. His hands were upon her, drawing back the upper folds of her nightdress, fondling her hair and pressing it to her quivering body. . .She was awake physically. Awake with a woman's desires, although she was only sixteen. . .And ghastly realization, was the increasing bestial instincts rising within her."

Sonia Wingfield shares a neurotic and introspective nature with the other young ladies. She suffers a degrading ecstasy. Lying in bed, she sees her other self keep a clandestine rendezvous, which leads to a ritual of torture which debases her at the same time it fascinates her. This time, the unsuspected villain is a young doctor (somewhat surprising, since most villains were usually advanced in years). He torments her as part of an experiment at creating a dual personality. He learned the secret from his father, who had experimented in like fashion on Sonia's mother.

As for Martha Lane, her guardian tries to debase her, just

as he had done to her mother, through drugs. It is the family physician who schemes to get Manya Corot's fortune. He tries to keep her from marrying, so he can continue as trustee. He fills her full of deadly drugs, as well as aphrodisiacs. She is subverted by her own lusting desires at the same time her lovers succumb to her death kisses. In much the same way, Landa Maine's guardian kills the men she scratches, to convince her she has caused their deaths.

Some of these stories carried the Ray Cummings byline; others were by Gabriel Wilson. (His wife's name was Gabrielle.) Some may have been written by her, or by both of them together, or by him alone. There was little difference in approach and treatment, in any case.

It seems that Cummings repeated his leitmotiv interminably. But it wasn't so often when measured against his total output. Donald Dale was more selective, with but two compositions on the same refrain: the sinister Prince Zagoul and his attempts to create art from death.

This unusual menace is first met in "The Beautiful Dead," in TERROR TALES (March-April, 1937). An art shop proprietor fears that his passion for a beautiful girl feeds only on her beauty; this obsession causes him to dream of defacing her, by peeling off her face for a death mask. The couple meet Prince Zagoul, who explains his theory of art. " 'Beauty at its zenith . . . is never inanimate . . . The nearer to life, the more beautiful. Objects of art are beautiful only in the degree to which they approach the animate.' " Later, the hero suffers a lapse, and finds himself with an unidentified, mutilated girl; his dream has come true and he realizes he can't control himself. He frustrates Zagoul's scheme to fashion a lifemask of the heroine's face. It was to have been a collaborative effort, in which he would once again have relived the dream, with his fiancee as victim. They escape.

But she is not safe. At any time in the future, his mania may return.

Prince Zagoul's further attempts at preserving perfection implicate a young sculptor, in "Art Class in Hell," in HORROR STORIES (June-July, 1937). His unwitting accomplice falls in love with a girl, an ideal-object, created from a crystal through his and Zagoul's combined wills. She wears an immense jewel, a counterpart of a flower that appeared in the crystal. It is Zagoul's intention to kill her and capture her innocent loveliness.

" 'I will drain the life from her body so subtly that, precisely at the crossing of the thin line that divides this world from the other, I will capture the last flutter of life and

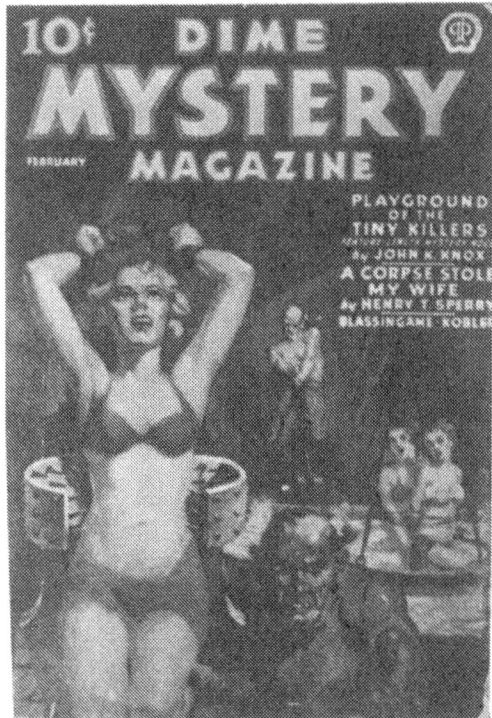

Won't they ever develop a new mise en scène? This one (February, 1938), with the figure in the foreground suffering the usual indignities, while the disconsolate damsels in the background apathetically await their fate at the hands of leering fiends, echoes the **Horror Stories** cover on page 104; both bear a resemblance to the **Terror Tales** on page 188.

Next question, anybody know what to do with fresh heads? It doesn't seem that there would be much use for them, not to mention, the rest of the body. This bit of gruesomeness appeared on the January, 1939 cover.

imprison it forever in the shell of her flawless beauty. That is art!' " So, now we find the base-minded scoundrel of earlier days replaced by the suave connoisseur of beauty. Once again, the villain is foiled, but this time, the hero finds his sweetheart's fate has only been temporarily delayed.

"Then I saw what I had not noticed before. The flower-like jewel on Zagoul's turban was identical with the one on Rhisa's breast!

" 'Watch! . . . She will be yours only so long as the champak blooms! . . .' Between his fingers he took one thin, flake-like leaf of the jeweled flower on his turban--and snapped it off . . . A sharp click! . . . Another!

"Before my dismayed eyes, a petal of the champak jewel on Rhisa's breast, as if snapped by an invisible hand, had broken off and fallen into the seething cauldron. There is only one petal left. When that is gone, I will lose Rhisa."

Whether describing a ravening monster from a mysterious pool, or a lascivious goat-man forcing his vile embraces on the helpless heroine, Dale's writing reflected one prevailing trait: virility. A reader surmised that the author must have been a regular hell-raiser, to have acquired all the out-of-the-ordinary facts and knowledge he made use of in his stories. What a surprise, then, when it was later revealed that Dale's real name was Mary Dale Buckner. Born in West Texas, she lived an out-of-the-ordinary life, but "hell-raising" didn't seem to have been a part of it. She said that she got her schooling from a certificate teacher who came to the family's ranch to live with them half the year. Later, she helped to self-educate herself by plowing through Caesar's Gallic Wars alone. She earned bachelor's and master's degrees at Texas Tech and was on her way to a Ph.D. when she started writing to meet expenses.

Thus, Dale belonged to a select company. While supernatural literature attracted many women writers, weird menacism didn't. In fact, only a few others can be found in these magazines. There was Frances Bragg Middleton. Like Dale, she was a facile exponent of the masculine point of view. A few others appeared once or twice. And there were a few husband-and-wife teams, like Edith and Ejler Jacobson.

Speaking of writing teams, Jacobson, or I should say, Jakobsson, passes along this word regarding working methods. "When we were battering away at the pulps, we had a small apartment in the Village. We put our desks as far away from each other as we could. We'd work awhile and then meet in the middle of the room to exchange pages. We went slowly. The fastest anything ever came out was a novelette in four days. We thought we were doing great."

CHAPTER XIV. THE SENSUOUS (SCIENCE FICTION) WOMAN

*It is nearly impossible to mix sex and
science fiction, any more than you can successfully mix sex and the supernatural.*

Groff Conklin
THE BEST OF SCIENCE FICTION

In 1952 a science fiction magazine called STARTLING
STORIES lived up to its name, with a novel by a new author.
The occasion was the appearance of "The Lovers," by Philip
José Farmer, and it created a furor. In fact, to some, this
tender account of an Earthman and his alien inamorata
smacked of heresy. Until the time the discovery was made
that women were built differently than men, and that these
differences could provide pleasure, the genre's idea of an
emotional attachment was an inventor doting lovingly on his
own handmade spaceship.

SF traditionalists might have been further shocked to have
come upon some of the material appearing in the weird
menace magazines nearly two decades earlier. There was a
good deal of suggestiveness back then, but this fact has
escaped the anthologizers, since the stories themselves have
remained so well hidden.

There were the Richard Tooker "Zenith Rand" space opera stories in MYSTERY ADVENTURES. Hardly imperishable classics, and fairly mild compared to some of the more unchaste selections available in other areas. Still, they were maybe half a light year ahead of mainstream SF, as far as dealing with provocative situations then. The hero, armed with his trusty long-barreled pyradine pistol, would be scouring the spaceways for his ardent Valkyria mate, who always ended up divested of most of her clothing and fleeing from all sorts of aroused other-worldly creatures, their mandibles gnashing and antennae waving frenziedly.

Then there was the strange combination of sex, sadism and science fiction served up by the Red Circle magazines. Popular, too, made sure its science fiction was stimulating. Developing science fiction concepts in the weird menace context led to interesting possibilities. Think about it a moment. You had the usual mystifying proceedings, in most cases, with a legitimate weird menace, ranging from world conquerors to infectious microorganisms (no more "mean old men going around in masks"), within a science fiction framework. The mixture wasn't a bad one. In addition, since most of the authors wrote little science fiction, they offered a change of pace and fresh viewpoint.

John Hawkins is an example. In "The Devil's Press-Agent," in HORROR STORIES (February-March, 1937) we come upon a mad scientist, no less, who menaces the world. The idea sounds hackneyed. But believe me, the treatment isn't. The style is mid-period BLACK MASK–cynical, depersonalized. The use of an unusual verbal voice prepares the reader at the beginning for the tragedy of death and a blighted life. That's known as a hooker. Hollywood does it often in movies, when one of the characters, who is later to die, lets fall a few broad hints about "not lasting," or "not making it," or something similar. In this case, it's more subtle.

A reporter and his wife are forced to serve a scientist, who wants to rule the world from his fortress, ringed by impulse barriers. The modified second person rendition at the beginning, followed by the first person--as the reporter tells his story--gives a sense of immediacy to the proceedings. The scientist has devised a huge power unit which "rips thunderbolts from the sinews of the sun." He boasts, " 'I can center my power on any spot on the globe. The calculations are already made for every capital city in the world. I can pluck the Eiffel Tower out of the guts of Paris or I can blast the whole city out of existence.' " The reporter finds a way to stop him, but at the cost of his wife's life.

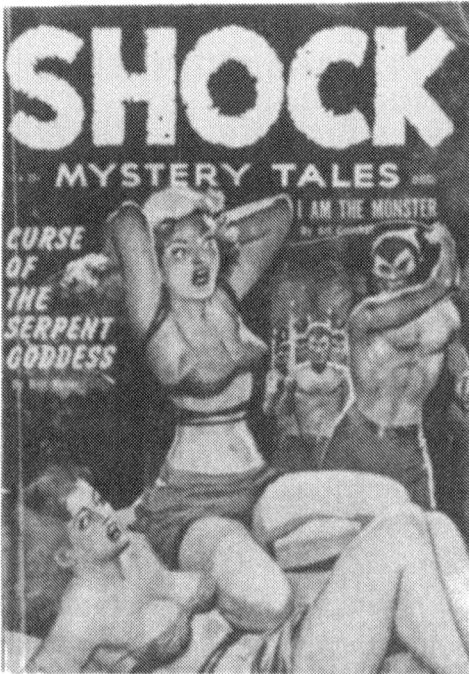

Here is an odd pulp: a weird menace attempt published in the sixties, long after that story style, and most pulps themselves, had left the scene. The stories were more travesties than serious weird menace, although the covers were in the usual tradition. This December, 1961 issue was digest-sized, instead of the pulp-size 6 3/4 x 9 3/4, had 128 pages, and sold for 35 ¢.

W. Wayne Robbins is not remembered for his science fiction output, if he's remembered at all. But he turned out some credible speculative fiction--with his "villains" amorphous, ravening entities. In one, a creature goes through a molecular change and begins growing, when a scientist feeds it the bodies of his wife and her paramour, whom he murdered. To appease it, the scientist tries to furnish other victims. On another occasion, the menace is an evolutionary substance, loosed from an urn discovered in the Gobi Desert. It infects the heroine's brother and directs him to infect others.

TERROR TALES called Robbins' "Test-Tube Frankenstein", "One of the most unusual novelettes we have ever printed," (May, 1940). Certainly, this was an old refrain. However, even being forewarned like this, and approaching the story with a skeptical attitude, you didn't feel let down. The gist is that the protagonist's friend is trying to nurture earthworm tissue. The two men observe a blob. The friend explains:

" 'That is as near as man has ever come to the pure, disembodied will to live . . . I can take it and crush it almost to shreds; I can immerse it in weak solutions of acids. But still it clings to whatever life it has in it. I built up that one instinct in it, practically to the exclusion of all others.' He laid a marble near one wall of the glass jar. For a moment nothing happened, but when it did, I had the impulse to rub my eyes. Because there were two marbles."

The scientist is done in by his own creation, when the mimic absorbs him, changing into his own outward image, down to his every mannerism. Its hunger grows. Searching for the hero, the monster assumes one form after another. The hero doesn't know who's real and who isn't--a dilemma that brings to mind Don A. Stuart's "Who Goes There?" The

Blondes on the buxom side were popular on covers during the late thirties, although the baddies never seemed to take the time to appreciate them. This November - December, 1939 issue was vintage sex-sadism, although the stylization had just about run its course by then.

creature's one limitation is that it can imitate only what it sees.

Obsessed with the urgency to kill the hero, the mimic adopts the form of his fiancee. It then attempts to trap him by partially disrobing, thus entice him near enough to seize him. But it had never seen a nude woman before.

"June swayed around, the subtle, willowy bend of her body so familiar, so normal, so dear to my every sense. And my eyes swept involuntarily over the gentle swell of her abdomen, up to the mellow contour of her breasts. There should have been a shy blush of pink at the tips. But there was nothing. I cried out; my eyes crawled from their sockets. No, smoothly ivory over their entire surface her breasts were without sign of nipple!"

You might say that the mimic's trick turned out to be a bust. While the eroticism in this story was mild, it was more than mainstream science fiction was giving its readers at the time. As a matter of fact, presenting science fiction in the weird menace pulps was a confounding business anyway. Some who did write science fiction now and then, such as Arthur Leo Zagat, Ray Cummings and Arthur J. Burks, did not turn out that kind of material for these magazines. Others did, but not under their own names. Edmond Hamilton took the name Robert Wentworth for "World Without Sex" in MARVEL TALES (May, 1940). This was one of the two sex-sadistic issues with that title. The plot has to do with the last males on earth escaping, after being condemned to death by the ruling matriarchal society. They kidnap some women, and plan forcible mating, in an atavistic return to male liberation. Still others, whose output was nearly all science fiction and fantasy, wrote neither, this time, but were promoted as if they had.

By October, 1962, **Shock** was larger than pulp size, 7-3/4 x 10-3/4, with 80 pages. There was a companion magazine called **Web Terror Tales,** but neither lasted long.

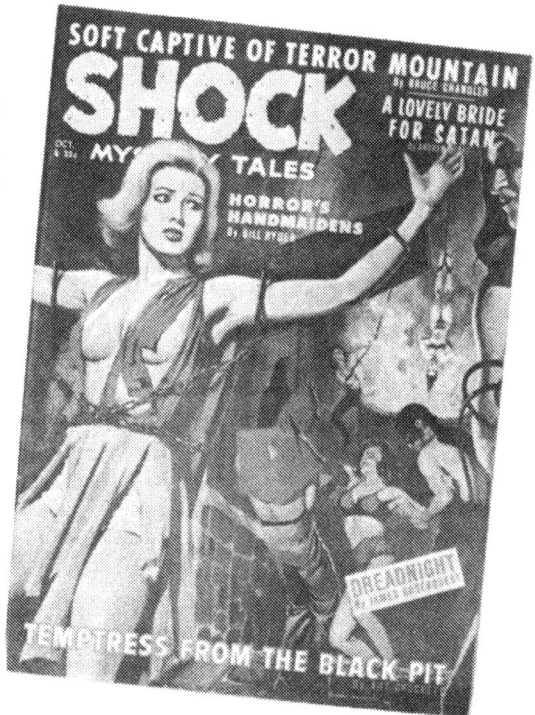

THRILLING MYSTERY printed several stories by such authors as Jack Williamson, Frank Belknap Long and Henry Kuttner, names to contend with in science fiction. Taking advantage of their reputation, the editor (with some connivance from the author) pretended that their stories were in this vein, probably figuring that this was a more compelling format, as far as the reader was concerned. It's not clear why they didn't just go ahead and write science fiction in the first place.

A Robot Leaves a Trail of Gruesome Corpses
Beneath Its Electric Sway!

Up to the final page, in fact, you kept believing it really was a robot (about the only science fiction touch, in any case), only to discover that the murderer was hiding in a

"Terror Is My Bride," by James Rourke, in **Mystery Novels and Short Stories,** July, 1940, is a title typical of so many—the suggestion of a weird relationship. In this case, the "bride" is the hero's belief that his fiancee killed someone, then his certainty that she's in danger, as he languishes in an insane asylum.

metal suit. In other words, the villain has simply shed his earlier monster costume for something a little more permanent. In another instance, you're led to believe that giant spiders are running amok, due to a biological experiment gone awry. Another disguise? Of course. Then there's the ethereal young lady brought to Earth from a frigid drifting mass in a solid stratum above the atmosphere, whose very nearness chills you to death. Except that the ice queen turns out to be an actress hired by the villain who does in his victims with liquid nitrogen. Shades of Batman's Mr. Freeze! To cite one more example, the invasion from the fourth dimension is brought about with a little luminous paint and a black cloth. The point here is that the science fiction writers weren't producing science fiction for the weird menace magazines, while the non-science fiction writers were.

Now, getting back to MARVEL TALES, the December, 1939 issue unveiled a curious blend of sex, sadism, the weird and bizarre, in science fiction format. Needless to say, this was the other weird menace issue. Both this one and the May number looked for all the world like other lurid Red Circles. One difference in makeup, though: each led off with a novel, a carryover from the preceding science fiction structure. Each was written by Nils O. Sonderlund. Unlike what went before, though, these were made purposely blatant--which would make you think that they must have been of little value. The novel that concerns us here, "Angel From Hell" (in the December issue) was anything but, despite the following unblushing blurb.

Amazing Book-Length Novel of a Lust-Mad
Earth-Man Horde That Pitted Super-Science
Against Eternity's Golden Bird-Girl!

After that preamble, it couldn't be anything but rampant immorality. But no, unlike other Red Circle offerings, this

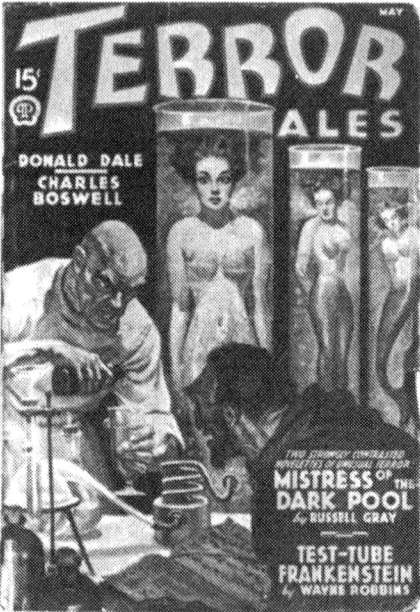

Science fiction-oriented covers were few and far between. This is the May, 1940 issue, with Wayne Robbins' fine "Test-Tube Frankenstein."

one keeps the passion prose to a minimum; there is no ostentation. It skillfully combines romantic adventure and sense-of-wonder. The story is divided between two protagonists. Carter Boyd is an American flier who saves an incredible golden bird-girl from attacking planes in the Gobi Desert. Jimmy Hall is a soldier-of-fortune. He has ostensibly been hired to fly for Chiang Kai-shek's government, but finds himself at odds with Balkan plotters (who bluster about with a Prussian accent) and Mongol spies. Switching back and forth, we enjoy an idealized, lyrical involvement between Boyd and the bird-girl, followed by a fast-moving and suspenseful melodrama with Hall pitted against a world conqueror. Alexander is what he calls himself. His weapons are G-bombs and a G-ray projector. He describes the projector.

" 'At a hundred miles, even, it can crush down a hostile plane with double its weight. At ten miles, it can crush men into dough, and make the solid earth flow like water to close the trenches over them, and cause battleships to sink as if a giant hand thrust them down!' "

Boyd and Hall, joined in a common cause, with a young girl, go to Alexander's beam station off the Siberian coast, to rescue the bird-girl, who had been captured and tortured. The G-ray strikes them down, as Alexander's men, in radiation-proof armor come for them.

"A satanic laugh echoed hollowly from the hooded head of Renvic. He came to the side of the girl. Kicking off his snowshoes, he drove his black boot roughly against her side . . .His boot came down savagely, upon the soft curves of her breast. She sobbed again, piteously."

These pulps didn't do much more than this with science fiction concepts. I don't know why. Of course, the inveterate science fiction reader would not have gone to these sources in the first place, for his reading pleasure, nor would he have cared much for having his "science" diluted with sex. But for the regular reader of such magazines, it must have been a welcome change of pace when the weird menace turned out to be a protoplasmic blob, for instance, instead of someone hiding behind a disguise.

CHAPTER XV. GOTHICISM'S LAST GASP

Clean-up organizations started to throw their weight around and gave editors the jitters, and artists and writers were instructed to put panties and brassieres on the girls.
Bruno Fischer
WRITER'S DIGEST (July, 1945)

The final years of the weird menace magazines saw several changes. ("Final years" in this context means 1940 and 1941.) Publishers tried to stave off declining readership returns, as some of their titles began floundering. Popular phased out sex-sadism at the same time the Red Circle magazines promoted it blatantly. New titles hit the stands as old titles of the same type disappeared. The pulp business as a whole, in fact, began retrenching at that time, in the face of increasing competition from comic books and pressure to clean up its product.

There's nothing wrong in change, of course. A good editor keeps his finger on the pulse of his public, and responds to any speedup or slowdown in tempo. He should be continually modifying and adapting. A static editorial course can result in a ship becalmed. But change in the pulps was never a gradual process. It was a case of using a bludgeon, not a rapier, to strike the customer's fancy. While these attacks on the reading public were conducted with ferocity and swiftness, at least, there was an attempt to make them respectable.

194

From the accompanying announcements, you'd think that the changes were the result of long deliberations involving at least the company president and his editorial director, if not the business manager, account director and switchboard operator. DIME MYSTERY is a case in point.

Remember the sudden shifts it made over the years? Following the defective detective phase, this public proclamation appeared (in the May, 1941 issue).

"Not until this issue have we been able to give you a full 100 percent sample of the magazine we always knew DIME MYSTERY could become."

In other words (according to the editor), many years of preparation went into this. Everything up to now has been aimed at this goal. In reality, the statement translates into this: "An issue or two ago, we decided to try something different." (In this case, detective mysteries--a sort of full-circle return to the earliest years). Decisions like this were usually made by the editor responsible for the publication, with the publisher practically a stranger to the day-to-day operation of the titles in his chain.

This latest change in DIME MYSTERY simply highlighted a condition that had come about a few years earlier: the expugning of the earlier self-conscious grandiloquence of the Gothic presentation. By then, the stories read more comfortably, were terse and generally more to the point. Going back further, we find a harbinger of this hard-hitting approach in a series of fact articles featured by Popular. In the July, 1937 issue, DIME MYSTERY inaugurated a series called "History's Gallery of Monsters." The author, John Kobler, is still active today. A few years ago, he served as editor-at-large for THE SATURDAY EVENING POST, when still owned by Curtis. Recent books of his are a biography of LIFE'S founder, the late Henry Luce, and his present study of Al Capone.

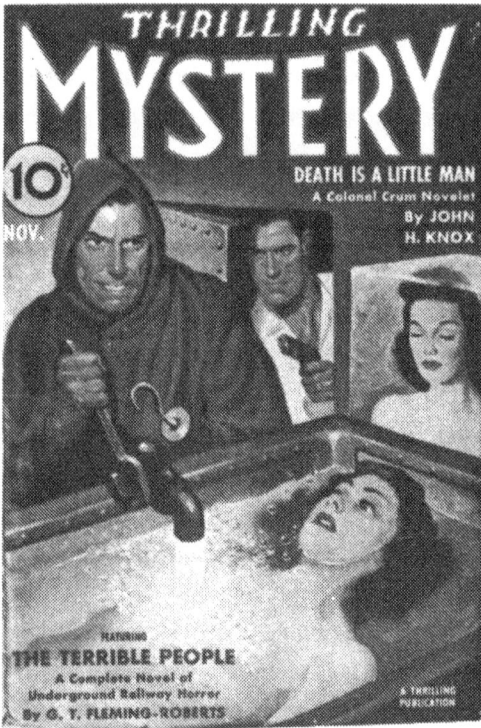

This girl getting the ice bath harks back to an earlier **Horror Stories** cover. Remember? This one is the November, 1940 issue, when such investigative heroes as Colonel Crum were being featured.

He wrote ten instalments of his series, biographing such deviants as Gaetano Mammone, the vampire bandit of Italy; Gilles de Rais, France's "Bluebeard;" Sawney Beane, head of a cannibalistic, cave-dwelling family; Peter Kurten, the child killer; and the lonely hearts murderess, Belle Gunness. A similar three-article series of his appeared in TERROR TALES, titled "Disciples of Death."

Charles Boswell wrote the longest-running series. His "Caravan of Incredible Crimes" ran in eleven issues of HORROR STORIES and one issue of TERROR TALES. Like the other selections, these dealt with poisoners, marriage murderers, stranglers, and baby killers. Today, Boswell's articles are seen in several current publications.

Both Kobler and Boswell performed credibly. There is little to choose between their styles. Even when somewhat pretentious, and obviously carried away by their own creative efforts, they could interject a certain amount of artistry, even humor, into their accounts. Here is an example from Boswell's chronicle of three killers, William Godfrey Youngman, Herman W. Mudgett and Thomas P. Fitzgerald.

"Not caring actually or actuarially whether its insureds die naturally or accidentally (unless there is a double indemnity clause), by another's hand or by their own (unless death occurs within the limits of the suicide clause), an insurance company is, however, taken aback when it learns that a policyholder has died by the ungrateful efforts of the one the policy was to protect.

"It was this ball of viciousness that Youngman tossed about and played with and finally put into effect, and then, dying, passed along to Mudgett--Mudgett the newborn. The infant proved apt and nursed it in his cradle with more care than he

himself was nursed and, on reaching manhood, batted it about with dexterity and such phenomenal strength as to surpass even his testator. Then Mudgett saw its reincarnation in the embryo of what was to become Fitzgerald--saw even as a noose cut off his powers of seeing. He passed it as one runner passes the relay to the next and Fitzgerald caught it up with agility."

How happy Popular's editors must have been to see this factual presentation under way. For years, they had been briefly documenting similar reprehensible deeds, to reinforce their oft-repeated refrain that the real world of violence was as incredible as the make-believe one in the magazines. Their point was that the authors weren't dreaming up anything that didn't or couldn't happen. These editorial program notes appeared in such appropriately titled departments in the three magazines as "Chamber of Horrors," "The River Styx," and "The Black Chapel."

Boswell's and Kobler's reports may have derived from an earlier series in THRILLING MYSTERY. The first issue of that publication presented "Horror-Scopes," conducted by Chakra, "the famous mystic." At that time, it promised to go "behind the scenes of mystery, taking readers into the power-house of life and watching the wheels go round." For awhile, Chakra wrote about unusual crimes, involving many of the people later written up in the Popular pulps. Soon, though, he concentrated on brief reports of seemingly unexplainable occurrences. Although he attested to their genuinness, he remained purposely hazy on names, places and dates. The column concluded each month with questions and answers relating to psychic phenomena.

Moving ahead to 1940, the year the final Boswell piece appeared, we come upon a new pulp entry. RED STAR MYSTERY (there's that word "mystery" again) was one of several new titles featuring the single-series hero the Munsey company tried. This one made a play for the super-hero cult and weird-menace clientele at the same time. . .and lasted four issues. Each one contained a fifty-five page novel about Don Diavolo, the Scarlet Wizard, written by Stuart Towne. The author's real name was Clayton Rawson. He died in 1971 at the age of sixty-four. He had appeared on the stage

10¢ **Red ★ Star** ᴬᵁᴳ·
Mystery

Murder Leaves No Trace—if the Killer is Invisible
DON DIAVOLO—The Scarlet Wizard
Faces His Most Baffling and Exciting Problem When He Meets
• BOOK—LENGTH NOVEL
Death Out of Thin Air   COMPLETE IN THIS ISSUE

Red Star Mystery (this is the August, 1940 issue) featured Don Diavolo in each of the four issues, for the super hero lover, and some weird shorts, for the horror buff. It was one of several Munsey Red Star titles, all soon acquired (but not continued) by Popular Publications.

as "The Great Merlini," and had written mysteries featuring this character. The short stories played around with the horror-terror idea, but didn't go over too well. Among the authors were John Knox, Frances Bragg Middleton, Richard Huzarski and G. T. Fleming-Roberts. It was during this time that the Munsey line found the going rough. The company sold out to Popular in 1942. Rogers Terrill, now an associate publisher there, took over ARGOSY, which was the main attraction. Within a year, ARGOSY had become a general illustrated monthly.

Meanwhile, THRILLING MYSTERY was image-changing too. Thrilling decided that the confused hero caught up in a weird mystery was all well and good. But there was nothing like a good old professional crime fighter to carry a story along. The magazine switched to a detective format in the early forties, although the change had started back in 1938.

That year, a novel began appearing in each issue--that is, a story of some sixteen thousand words or so. The hero was an investigative type. Other stories also utilized private detectives, as well as that popular pulp folk-hero, the newspaperman. But the stories still emphasized weird menace. There were overtones of voodooism, lycanthropism and vampirism--all part of the usual attempt at misdirection on the author's part, of course. Murder was still bloody, with heads chopped off and hearts torn out. However, the earlier dragged-out lurid description had been toned down almost to a reportorial dispatch.

"For suddenly the jaws of a vise wrenched sharply in a short arc. There was a grinding snap and crunch--and Jimmy Parker's knees collapsed like a deflated tire, as black oblivion claimed his last spark of life."

A year or so earlier, the business of doing away with the victim brought to the fore all the author's talents for prolonging nauseating descriptions. Now, though, the emphasis was on personal characteristics.

"Iron Brandt they called him. There were two hundred pounds of that metal in him, heated with liquor, hammered with bullets, tempered in gore. In another era he might have been a feudal lord, or a swashbuckling buccaneer. Instead, he was a private detective, a ruthless bloodhound of a man."

Just when it looked like some real shuddery situation was developing, the author might sidestep the issue. For instance, a couple take refuge from a storm in a lodge. (They never learn, do they?) Masked men overpower them. This dire threat is made:

" 'You are in the House of Fiends! An unbidden guest at the Fiends' Club, of which the master is leader. Men and women who find their only pleasure in these weekly sadistic revels. Tonight you will lose a wife or sweetheart. And in losing her, you will experience the exquisite agony of witnessing death at its worst.' "

Except for a possible minor disgruntlement at the villain's grammatical shortcomings, the reader certainly had reason to look forward to a few choice depravities: at the least, a turn or two on the rack, or some digs from the Iron Maiden. A Donald Graham, at this point, wouldn't have hesitated to fling the heroine off a heated platform kerplunk on sharpened spikes, or to nail her to an inverted cross, to be mercilessly whipped by sniveling and snorting old lechers. But what happens here? A reluctant boa constrictor is brought in and has to be forced to make advances toward the heroine.

Yes, a good deal of the offensiveness (or verve, depending on your viewpoint) had gone out of the stories. The result was sometimes a more believable buildup, and an element of human interest. "Hate's Havoc," by Bernard Breslauer (March, 1940) is a vivid psychological tale on a much more personal level than, say, John Knox's "Nightmare," to cite one of the few other examples of this type that comes to mind. Deirdre is convinced that Tom has switched his affections to her sister, Benita. Death visits her and says, " 'Deirdre, what you seek, you shall have. Benita bloodless.' " He makes all three small and puts them into bottles. A gigantic surgeon appears, to draw the blood from Benita. Tom shatters the glass to go to the rescue of Deirdre, and in the process, breaks the shackles of her mind. She is cured of her obsession. Later her psychiatrist explains to Tom what happened.

" 'It became clear to me, after several sessions with Deirdre, that unless the emotions of mingled hate and love which she was repressing could find an outlet, an incipient psychotic case would progress to an active psychosis.' " He prepared her for Death's visit through hypnosis. A drug kept her at a level of consciousness that would allow her to believe in what she thought she saw. Her physician then brought in his puppets-- a hobby of his--to simulate the small figures. The act of Tom breaking free and going to her, not Benita, fulfilled her desire and cured her. The terrors of the mind are the most frightening. It's too bad more attempts at psychological horror, like this effective piece, weren't made by authors.

By the November, 1941 issue, THRILLING MYSTERY was carrying the legend, "Best Action Detective Stories" on the cover, while the spine still retained, "Weird Thrills on Every Page." At that time the magazine was bi-monthly, and had been since 1937. In this period, John Knox was chronicling the adventures of his scientific sleuth, Colonel Fabian Crum. Now the magazine was beginning to use the series character. Crum was a small man, described as "gnome-like." He had an assistant, Aga Aslan, who was "a swart-faced giant, like some jinn from the Arabian Nights." There was an odd couple for you.

The Trailer-Detective Probes
the Mystery of the Cave of
Snakes When Men Are Lured
to Tragic Death!

That's the redoubtable
Colonel Crum leading
the way, and depicted
larger than John Knox
described him. He was
one of the series crime
fighters in late issues of
Thrilling Mystery, this
story being, "The
Cyclops' Eye," in the
January, 1941 issue. He
made his debut in the
magazine two issues
earlier.

In 1942, George Chance, the Green Ghost, took up residence in THRILLING MYSTERY, after having had his own publication for seven issues. He was the magician-detective creation of G. T. Fleming-Roberts. Like such hardy souls as Frederick C. Davis (OPERATOR #5), Norman Daniels (THE BLACK BAT, THE SKIPPER) and Norvell Page (THE SPIDER), Fleming-Roberts found no difficulty in whipping out thousands of words a month of varying story lengths, in addition to carrying a super hero or two. He also wrote The Black Hood series (three stories). To mention a later period, in 1949, when the super hero had departed the pulps to all practical purposes, Popular unaccountably saw fit to bring out Fleming-Roberts' CAPTAIN ZERO. This was the most anti-establishment crime fighter of all time: clumsy, nearsighted and forgetful. The three novels provided something that had been missing before, in the deadly serious business of glamorizing super-hero perfection: that is, humor. In 1943 THRILLING MYSTERY went quarterly. Other investigator types in the final years included Private Detective McGee, Detective George Clayton, Press Agent Breckenridge Barnum and Unofficial Jones, spy fighter. The company was expanding its comic book business at the time, with such titles as (what else) THRILLING COMICS (Dr. Strange), and STARTLING COMICS. And with war-time paper shortages, much of the available woodpulp went into Thrilling's Popular Library paperback operation.

By adopting different formats, both THRILLING MYS-TERY and DIME MYSTERY put off the day of reckoning for awhile, even though the pulp business was finding the going rough as the war started. There were signs that all was not well, as seen in the increasing use of reprint stories and illustrations. Total company circulation in some cases was still healthy. Audited Bureau of Circulation figures show one and a half million for Popular, and one and a fifth million for Thrilling, in 1942. These two companies were in the best shape. Other publishers were nearing their pulp end. In a way, it seems that as the weird menace pulps left the scene in 1941, the pulp business as such went into its decline. It wasn't apparent to everyone. Even when the war caused massive cutbacks in woodpulp use, Leo Margulies was prophesying a bigger than ever resurgence in pulps afterwards.

As the emphasis shifted from murder as a black art, to

murder as a fine art, readers made known their displeasure. One complained:

"I am not really interested in the efforts of the hero to untangle and foil the machinations of the villain. All I want-- and am not getting--is the old, smashing climax scene with the characters wallowing in blood and the screams of the heroine and her pals rising to the heavens as the mad monsters prepare to do their worst."

Another reader, also in DIME MYSTERY, asked for "stories that make me shudder and make me tremble every time the telephone or doorbell rings." This drew the editorial aphorism: "We think you've got something there. There's a lot of good sense and sound psychology in what you say and we'll do our best to give you what you want." Editors came and went; new authors arrived; old ones left; the magazines changed in contents and appearance, but one immutable editorial law persisted: reading these nerve-jolters had thera- peutic value. You could just see the editor eagerly opening his mail, panting for the chance to pounce on this idea. How about a modern manifestation of this notion, say, as an ad on television?

"When you get that happy, perked-up feeling, and nothing bothers you, take a pulp break. Restore a balance to your life. Read the latest horror stories in your favorite magazine . . .and feel out of sorts, despondent and nervous again."

It's fitting that the company that started the weird menace boom in the thirties outlasted its competition to end it in the forties. MYSTERY NOVELS AND SHORT STORIES and the three Red Circle titles, REAL MYSTERY, UNCANNY TALES and MYSTERY TALES didn't get beyond the year 1940. THRILLING MYSTERY, of course, underwent a detective metamorphosis. But HORROR STORIES and TERROR TALES not only made it into 1941, but reinstituted briefly the weird menace stereotype that had appeared earlier. At the same time, the company expanded its line, in an abortive attempt to flail a dying horse. It was Gothicism's last gasp.

Traditionally, Popular had paid a minimum of one cent a word, with some authors receiving higher rates. In mid-1938, the company's BIG BOOK WESTERN was the only Popular pulp under this rate. Then in 1939, the company set up a publishing adjunct, called Fictioneers, Inc., using the printing address in Chicago instead of the editorial address in New York. Alden H. Norton, a long-time editor in the New York office, was put in charge of the new publishing venture. (He was still with the company at the time it was recently sold.) Fictioneers offered authors one half cent a word, thus setting a precedent for Popular. The idea was to establish a lower paying market that wouldn't jeopardize Popular's position. So while some pulp publishers around this time were developing a comic book line, Popular was expanding its pulp string.

In 1940, the year Fictioneers took over BLACK MASK, two new titles made their debut, selling at fifteen cents each. They were STARTLING MYSTERY and SINISTER STORIES, both edited by Costa Carousso. As was typical of pulps in this period of economy measures, they had one hundred and twelve pages, instead of the earlier one hundred and twenty-eight. Neither lasted long--two issues of STARTLING MYSTERY and three of SINISTER STORIES --even though Fictioneers proved a profitable venture for Popular during the forties. Cost-cutting was evident in the reprint covers they used, picked up from earlier HORROR STORIES and TERROR TALES; inside illustrations also were reprints--the only work involved there being the attempt to match picture with story. But surely all this had a detrimental effect on sales. The pulp buyer may not have

Here we see another reprint cover, in this case (February, 1940), taken from the September-October, 1938 issue of **Terror Tales.**

remembered specifically where he had seen the artwork. However, he wouldn't have needed a long memory to recognize something familiar there, possibly leading him to the conclusion that he had already read the stories. So now the pulps were in their reprint phase. DIME MYSTERY used earlier Popular covers, on nine issues during 1940. The Spicy line began running early stories again, retitled, and with new illustrations and bylines, to confuse the reader. And soon, the Goodman brothers, Martin and Abraham, and Louis Silberkleit ran into trouble with the Federal Trade Commission regarding reprints. The Federal Trade Commission obtained a cease and desist order against Silberkleit's Columbia Publications (the Double Action group) and the Goodmans' Newsstand Publications (including Western Fiction Publishing Co. and Manvis Publications). Henceforth, the two companies promised not to use reprints unless so indicated.

It's puzzling why Popular at that time tried not one but two new weird titles. Both HORROR STORIES and TERROR TALES were floundering, yet the company saw fit to make another stab at the mystery lover, and with an economy package, at that. In the first issue of SINISTER STORIES (February, 1940), the editor showed an awareness of the influence behind DIME MYSTERY some seven years earlier, with the promise of "sense-shocking horror of the type which has until now been reserved for the patrons of the Grand Guignol in Paris. . ." Then he blithely ignored what had been going on later (in his own company's publications, no less) by referring to SINISTER STORIES as "the only magazine of its type available." Such statements aren't surprising. HORROR STORIES in 1939 called itself the "oldest, most popular magazine specializing in chills," when of course both DIME MYSTERY and TERROR TALES preceded it. Never let it be said a pulp editor allowed facts to stand in the way of fiction. There wasn't much memorable from SINISTER STORIES or STARTLING MYSTERY. In some of the selections could be found the weird approach set against a Gothic background.

"The familiar valley seemed subtly charged with eerie menace, the rampart of hills that edged it, glowered down upon her. Her nerves were decidedly on edge, she told herself stormily. . .She laughed shortly at her newly acquired fears, but her laugh was weak and unconvincing. She shrank from its feeble sound as it punctured the still night air."

Authors had to stretch descriptions such as these out for several pages to make that half-cent-a-word rate pay off. The contents encompassed several styles. It's hard to determine just what readership they were aimed at. In some cases, a half-hearted attempt was made at stirring up the reader, although there was little sadism.

"His skeleton hand swooped down, captured her exposed white breast. Then his face, parchment yellow and evil, moved down to her. . .She had one hand over the wound on her abdomen, the other arm was flung across her breasts in a futile effort to hide them from the lusting stare of her captor."

A few selections stand out. Very reminiscent of the earlier story of dread, Hugh Cave's "School Mistress for the Mad," in SINISTER STORIES (April, 1940), shows the author's fine touch at suspenseful buildup. Diabolicism, that's the word to describe the effect he achieved. In this one, a young school teacher in a backwoods farm area suffers recurrent headaches while trying to handle her moronic pupils. The headaches, of course, are part of a plot, by a doctor experimenting at subjecting a person's will.

One of Russell Gray's most polished weird shorts also appeared in SINISTER STORIES (February, 1940). "Song of Evil Love" has a pianist fall under the influence of a ravishing creature, "dark with smoldering black eyes and a body which no man could keep from looking at twice." She entraps him through a "hellish melody" she plays.

Meanwhile, HORROR STORIES and TERROR TALES were alive but not well. Covers had been toned down drastically, with the miscreants now fleshy yeggs and Hollywood Grade B heavies. The smirking and lurking demons of days gone by had turned into ordinary toughs. Needless to say, the heroines had their clothes back on. Inside, what do we see, but the Gothic tale once more, burning fitfully like a guttering candle in a decaying mansion. But if we look closer, we see a spark of life. It is in this final period that one of Francis James' best stories is found. He had been a frequent contributor to publications of this type for years. Editors thought highly of him, since he usually rated cover mention, and even such exclamations as **Francis James Is Back!** But as an author, he was more careless than most, often ignoring plausible resolutions completely. However, his "Scourge of the Faceless Men" in HORROR STORIES (December, 1940) has a breathless pace to it and a sense of melodrama. It depicts a city in bondage, prey to a pestilential plague. A virulent epidemic of leprosy is striking indiscriminately. An enigmatic doom-man offers salvation at a price. To the inhabitants, this represents their only hope, as the beleagured city has been quarantined by National Guard units dug in around the perimeter, with orders to shoot anyone trying to escape.

The heroine is about to dispatch the hero in this scene from George Vandegrift's "White Mother of Shadows," **Terror Tales,** January, 1941. But despite the voodoo trappings, it's just a case of drugs, and fortunately, they wore off before any irreparable damage was done.

In its evocation of irrevocable fate, this story harkens back to the Gothic period of some five years earlier. In fact, in mood and treatment, it shares a close affinity with Nat Schachner's "Creatures of the Dusk," in TERROR TALES (July, 1935), and may have been inspired by that account of a city terrorized by dead-alive creatures. Compare the way each begins.

Schachner's: It was past nine o'clock and already quite dark when Dean Madison drove into Compton Village. Fear rode at his side, a pallid companion, clutching his arm with a death-cold grip, forcing him to breakneck speed.

Now James': The voice came from darkness that plugged the vestibule like solid ink. Joan whimpered and grabbed my arm. I could feel her fear. I could smell it. The night was a miasma of terror.

Whatever redeeming or socially significant entertainment value these magazines had, they couldn't put off the evil day. TERROR TALES ended in March, 1941, and HORROR STORIES the following month. It's been said the censors had a hand in the demise of the weird menace pulps. Certainly, there had been pressure on publishers to expugn offensive material from their magazines. William R. Cox has commented on this. He wrote the Tom Kincaid series and several other popular crime stories in the forties.

"It was then that Rog Terrill decided to alter the contents of DIME MYSTERY, mainly due to the fact that Mayor La Guardia was sniffing around the newsstands looking for pornography. . .Imagine the poor Little Flower today!"

The Spicies, particularly, found the going tough in New York City. It's been said that La Guardia wouldn't let them in unless the covers were removed, and they were sold under the counter. Spicy became Speed in the early forties, to take some of the heat off.

Other factors were at work, too. Book publisher Karl Edward Wagner makes this pertinent observation.

"As to the failure of the sex and sadism and weird menace pulps, I believe a lot of it was due to the social pressures of the pre-war years. There was a definite aura of moral permissiveness and thrill-seeking to the thirties; perhaps the Depression had lent a darker note to the wild gaiety of the twenties. By the forties the inevitable backlash had set in-- and along with it a popular wave of moral puritanism that characterizes a society on the brink of war (just as the reverse characterizes the aftermath of war).

"Nor can the triteness of the formula plots be said to have glutted their audience. Readers don't really care about this, as witness the success of Doc Savage and other formula-written stories, and the hackneyed porn novels of today. Basically, the tastes of the reading public were changing due to a change in the social aura of the times, and the market for these pulps had gone dry."

So we've reached the end of the weird menace line. It came as the pulp publishing business itself began retrenching. Production costs were rising. Distribution problems arose. And the newsstand display space was being taken over by the hero in cape and tights. That is to say, comic books were becoming big business. From sixty titles in 1940, they jumped to one hundred and sixty-eight in 1941, and reached 100,000 newsstands. Where such publishers as A. A. Wyn in 1939 couldn't top six hundred thousand circulation for his dozen or so titles listed in his advertising group, the Detective Comics unit (including ACTION, ADVENTURE and MORE FUN) in 1940 went over 820,000 for four titles. That year the Fox Comic Group reached a million in sworn circulation. And advise, the comics were more profitable, too. Remember what a black and white ad in the pulps brought? It was in the neighborhood of $1,200 for an appearance in anywhere from ten to sixteen issues simultaneously. A black and white in the comics, to appear in only four concurrent issues, netted the company around a thousand dollars.

After the war, some forty publishers turned out some six hundred comic books, with a total circulation of 60 million —at least four times what the pulps' total circulation was in the thirties for any given month. (We're talking about circulation, not readership, here. Readership is always higher.) Those were the facts of publishing life, then. It didn't take elaborate surveys to show what the trend was. To sum up, there was more gold in the four-color comics panel, than in the black and white pulp word.

The final issue of **Horror Stories,** April, 1941, has the heroine clothed, and shows a deterioration in cover artistry, although the event is weird enough, certainly.

EPILOGUE

Printed on paper made (apparently) from gray oatmeal, pressed between illustrated covers seven times too vivid to be called garish and shipped in carload lots to all points of the English-speaking compass.
Henry Morton Robinson
THE BOOKMAN, August 1928

By now, it's obvious that only a vigorous constitution could withstand the demands of the pulps. I'm speaking of writing them, not reading them, although physical stamina might well apply in both cases. Grinding out story after story, day after day, required a great degree of physical hardihood. But no less important was a nimble mind. No one could call a pulp author slow-witted. In fact, in some of the stories--particularly in the weird menace line--the devious plot twists are so smooth and intriguing, you can't help but admire the mentality that devised them. Of course, if things came unstuck at the end . . . well, maybe the author simply had lost interest by then. Or more likely, since he had accomplished his purpose, that of shivering the reader's timbers, why bother to put any more effort into it? But the sheer prose skill is evident, in any case.

So it should come as a surprise now, to learn that pulp authors had a secret failing, so far, not publicly noted. Even more surprising, they made a point of cultivating it, in a sort of reverse-autosuggestive Couéism. It was this: Every day in

214

every way, I am forgetting more and more. Yes, that's right. They deliberately made themselves forget--not how to write, but what they had written. In other words, pulp authors have the world's worst memories. They can't tell you the titles of their stories, when they were written, or even, what they were about. This goes a long way in explaining why it's so difficult now to get inside information about the pulp writers and their stories. I've quoted several authors so far, who did provide personal data from those bygone times. But when pressed, few today could come up with intimacies about their own output, much less anyone else's. This fact became clear long before this present work was begun.

But it took a personal visit recently to three authors, to uncover the reason for this creative deficiency. It was Paul Ernst who made the startling admission. He said that a pulp writer, to survive, had to forget everything he wrote. That was the only way that what you said the day before wouldn't get in the way of what you were saying today. Wyatt Blassingame seconded this observation. And when you think about it, it makes sense. I had just never thought about it before.

Both Ernst and Blassingame have had their say here earlier, with general observations about the pulp business. In Blassingame's case, since he wrote "how-to-do-it" articles at the time, we have a better idea about his approach. What follows gives additional personal insight into how an author works. Joining them is a third author, Baynard Kendrick. This detective and mystery writer is new to this history, although BLACK MASK readers will recognize him. While he did very little in the horror-terror field, he experienced the vagaries common to all pulp writers--and vividly recalled some for me. All three live within 200 miles of each other in Florida.

The first stop was to see Baynard Kendrick, founder and first president of Mystery Writers of America. The directions to his house were to turn at the trailer sales sign, go past the old English church, bear left at the academy, and stop at the yard with the two wagon wheels. This was typical of many Florida communities that have sprung up near cities: you give directions by landmarks, not street names.

Kendrick is a bluff, hearty eighty years old. For most of his adult life, he has been interested in the plight of the blind. His blind detective, Captain Duncan Maclain, has enjoyed a good deal of success in book form. Another book, *Lights Out*, was made into the movie, "Bright Victory," with Arthur Kennedy winning the best actor award for his portrayal of a blinded soldier. Another detective, Miles Standish Rice, appeared in both book form and in BLACK MASK, which bought "the 20,000-word novelettes at a cent and a half or I never could have gotten by," he wrote in an autobiographical sketch. "The first Stan Rice appeared in an issue with my name on the cover together with those of Leslie Charteris and Erle Stanley Gardner, both old and very dear friends."

A boyhood chum from his hometown of Philadelphia was blinded while serving with the Canadians during World War I. Kendrick, also serving with Canada, visited him at St. Dunstan's, a charity hospital in London. While there, he observed a blind soldier who had a remarkable ability to tell him things about himself that even a person who could see might not have noted. This so impressed Kendrick that it was still vivid in his memory twenty years later, and became the inspiration of his Maclain novels. Asking Kendrick to comment on his writing days and the people he knew elicited the following:

"I'm probably best known for the series on Captain

Duncan Maclain. Only one story appeared in the pulps, in DIME DETECTIVE, as a serial. I got $1500 for it. He appeared in REDBOOK and AMERICAN MAGAZINE, and in twenty books." ("Longstreet" was based on the series on television just last year.)

"I've been in thirty-five magazines, pulps and slicks. My main markets were BLACK MASK and DETECTIVE FIC-TION WEEKLY. Captain Joseph T. Shaw was the editor of BLACK MASK when I started, and then Fanny Ellsworth took it over when he died. She was Mrs. Jack Davis, and Jack Davis was an editor at Munsey's for quite a while.

"The first thing I ever sold was to FIELD & STREAM, in 1926. I was general manager for Bing and Bing's Hotels at that time, in New York. I was let out of Bing and Bing's a week before Christmas in 1931, and I said I'd never work for anyone again. So I wrote three books and made $270 out of the three. That was when I got into the pulps.

"The pulps were feeding money. I could do a 20,000-word novelette when I was writing in Hartford, get on the train and take it down to New York, have lunch with Fanny Ellsworth and get a check after lunch. That's why the pulp writers stayed with them. They paid you. You could die of old age before you ever heard from COSMOPOLITAN. Some of the others were the same way.

"I wrote two books in a coal cellar in Astoria. There was no heat, just pipes running overhead. The rats scuttled back and forth on the pipes. I wrote during the day, with three or four Italian kids with their noses pressed against the window watching me.

"Then I went down to Florida and turned out *The Iron Spiders*, a Stan Rice story. Most of my early books were written in Florida. Stan Rice was a Florida investigator for the state's attorney's office. He appeared in books and in novelettes. Unfortunately, I became a collector's item. There's nothing that can ruin a writer like becoming a collector's item. I can't find any of my books. I don't even have all of them. Today, your markets are all gone. Why, I could count on three novelettes a year from AMERICAN MAGAZINE. You could live on three novelettes from them nicely, without doing anything else.

"I knew Arthur Leo Zagat. Gardner, Oscar Schisgall, Zagat and I had dinner at a little French restaurant on Madison Avenue two nights before Leo stepped out of his car and dropped dead. I knew Paul Ernst and still do. I knew Steve Fisher. I always told Paul he wrote a thousand stories. He turned out a 50,000-word novelette and four short stories under different names a month for years. Steve Fisher sent telegrams to all the movie companies, saying, 'Latch on to Steve Fisher, up and coming,' and signed, W. Somerset Maugham. They invited him out. That's how he got started there. Oh, he was a mad man. He made a lot of money in Hollywood.

"Talk about electric typewriter boys. I guess George F. Worts was at the top of the heap. William Clayton, the publisher, wrote about Worts coming up to his place. He had a big home in Nyack and invited George Worts for a weekend. He had servants and everything. George came with his tent and pitched it out on the grounds and brought his own steaks and whiskey. Clayton never got over this. He said, 'Well, George, I expect to feed you.' Worts replied, 'I'm very particular where I eat; I bring my own food.' And he grilled the steaks right out on the grounds in front of the Clayton mansion.

"Worts took a course at Columbia under Walter B. Pitkin, who wrote, *Life Begins at Forty*. Worts was a very meek and mild little guy. He sat in the back of the class. He turned in a story. Pitkin read it as an example of the worst thing ever written. Then he said, 'But why didn't I stop at the beginning?' Worts never said who he was. He had sold at least $75,000 worth to the pulps at that time. 'Let's consider this story,' Pitkin continued. 'It's the worst I've ever read in my life. But why couldn't I put it down?' That must be the answer. The English may have been bad, and the plot may have been terrible, but you couldn't put a good pulp story down. Worts wrote every type, from love to detective. He turned out 25,000 words a day. He died with an unfinished manuscript on the table beside his hospital bed. He had done two thirds of the story, reaching out of bed, so weak he could hardly push the keys.

"I ran into Lester Dent at the Tortilla, on 44th Street, one morning. I went there for breakfast. Lester said, 'Baynard, I see you've started this Mystery Writers of America. I want to join.'

"I said, 'Well, come on it; we'd love to have you.'

" 'But I've never written anything but the pulps.'

" 'Neither have any of us,' I said.

" 'How the hell do you break into these slick magazines?' he asked.

" 'What do you want to break into them for? You're making more money than any writer going. You've never been out of LaPlata, Missouri."

" 'I'm never going to move. I have my boat in Miami and I commute. Winters I go down to Miami and live on the Bugeye, and then I go home.'

" 'What do you average?'

" 'Two fifty to three hundred a week.'

" 'Why do you stay in LaPlata?'

" 'I'm the goddamnest biggest toad in the smallest puddle in the United States. Everybody in town bows and says, How are you, Mr. Dent? If I moved to New York I'd be lost with jerks like you.'

"He only lived a few years after joining the Mystery Writers, and then died. And then Raymond Chandler was president for three months and died.

"I earned $300 to $400 a month during the Depression. I'm not fast but I guess I'm prolific, with forty-four books under my belt. But it took me just as long to write a pulp story as it did a slick story. When I broke into AMERICAN MAGAZINE, where you got $4000 to $5000 for a 20,000-word novelette, I dropped the pulps in a hurry. Just like Paul Ernst quit them completely, when he started writing for REDBOOK and COSMOPOLITAN.

"One of my pulp stories that made quite a hit was one where they burned the panties off the girls with a blowtorch. Those were hard to write. Hell, you don't think I'd put my own name on a thing like that? They changed the title. You lost everything when you sold a horror story."

Burning the panties off girls was a typical diversion found in the weird menace stories. But it wasn't for the likes of Paul Ernst, who depended more on solid plotting than shocking situation. Today, Ernst's dark hair and youthful outlook belie his seventy-odd years. He looks ahead, not back, he's quick to point out. While this is a positive attitude, it's particularly frustrating for a delver into pulp arcana of the past, since Ernst had little interest in recalling his own experiences.

During his heyday, Ernst wrote for most of the pulp markets, with his weird output alone as extensive as many another's total production. The Ernsts got married on the money paid for his serial, "The Black Monarch," which began in the February 1930 issue of WEIRD TALES. For thirty years, they lived in Bucks County, near Philadelphia, before moving to Florida. There they owned an old farmhouse that they renovated. To pay for the cost, Ernst wrote several stories (around 1936) which had to do with farms and old rural homes--his rustic horror period, you might say. In one, an evil entity inhabits an old cistern, menacing the hero and his wife. In another example, a young couple moves into an old farm house, reputed to be hexed. This time the nemesis (the devil himself) resides in a strange chimney, that seems to have no direct outlet. From there, he steals forth, eventually spiriting away the wife. Within a few years--in 1939, that is-- Ernst was developing a different theme, in his super-hero period. I'm speaking, of course, of THE AVENGER, the Man of Steel, visualized by Street & Smith as a companion to the popular DOC SAVAGE, the Man of Bronze. Both appeared under the Kenneth Robeson byline, and both were written with the same facile, ingratiating style, although by different authors, of course. Ordinarily, THE AVENGER would not be taken up here. But some of Ernst's comments referred to this character, and therefore, seem worth including.

"I wrote four days a week, 5,000 words a day, for fifty-two weeks a year--a million words a year, from 1934 to 1940. I worked from nine in the morning until one thirty. I learned to do it right the first draft. It was letter perfect. I got an idea, sat down at the typewriter, numbered page one, and proceeded from there. I sold ninety percent of my material. But I never read anything I wrote. I had no interest in it. You could throw it out the window, as long as I got the check. When I wrote science fiction, it was just a wisp of science built around the weird.

"I was doing a lot for Street & Smith, going to New York once a week from Bucks County. John Nanovic asked me to do the character thing. I said no. He quoted a figure. 'Look, we'll even give you the idea.' I said okay. They paid me

$750 a novel, for THE AVENGER. I didn't copy Dent's style, though. Henry Ralston, one of Street and Smith's vice presidents, gave me the plots. I don't know whether he gave Walter Gibson his ideas for THE SHADOW or not but I suspect he did. THE AVENGER was probably the poorest writing I've ever done.

"When I was writing for the pulps, I trained myself to forget. You can't be thinking of an idea you did the day before, when you're trying to write something new. You'll ruin what you're trying to do, otherwise. I must have done a good job of it, since I can't remember any of the stories I wrote. You mentioned 'The Avenger's' personal tragedy in the first novel about him. I can't remember that at all. It's a complete blank. You mentioned his aides. I don't recall a one. But from what you say, the stories sound rather interesting. Maybe I should read one sometime . . . Today, I write one novelette a year for GOOD HOUSEKEEPING; when that magazine goes, I'll be fully retired."

And in this casual way, Ernst dropped his bombshell: he made himself forget everything he ever wrote, just as others did too. His amnesiacal attitude may have been dictated by the exigencies of fast-moving story telling. But it's hard to believe that he could have put something so completely from his mind, something that required his full attention a good part of the day, and provided him with his livelihood for so many years.

Ernst's low opinion of his own work calls to mind George Raft's comment about his own films. "I've never seen one of them; I never wanted to." In Ernst's case (and in Raft's), his own evaluation is suspect. THE AVENGER is a well-written, colorful saga that ranks at the top of the single-hero-type adventure series, to my way of thinking. I might say that just about all his other stories are equally enjoyable.

Continuing the movie-actor analogy, the third person I visited, Wyatt Blassingame, bore a strong resemblance to Lionel Stander, except that his pleasant Southern intonation is unlike Stander's harsh inflection. Getting to his house, too, was a matter of counting turns. He and Ernst know each other, although they don't socialize, while Kendrick and Ernst keep up their acquaintanceship by telephone. Unlike Ernst, Blassingame showed neither reluctance in recalling his writing days, nor displeasure over his pulp achievements. Like Ernst, though, he early learned that surprising trick of making himself forget what he had written. "Yes, you have to, or else what you said before will influence you later." Fortunately, he still remembers many details.

"We came down here in 1936 for the winter, and have stayed here ever since. I haven't done any fiction . . . let's see. I did a fiction piece about two years ago; it didn't sell in this country; it sold in England. That's about the only recent fiction I've done. I write an occasional magazine article. I did one for the AUDUBON MAGAZINE recently, on the dredge and fill problems in north Florida. I do occasional travel pieces. If you want to go somewhere, you want it off your taxes. Not long ago I did two articles for FORD TIMES and another for TRAVEL AND LEISURE. Ford pays $400 for about a thousand words. TRAVEL AND LEISURE is even better, if you can get into the international issue. The last piece was a thousand words, and brought in $500, plus $250 expenses.

"Short stories are really a young man's business. Once you become acutely aware of the plots, you begin to realize how often you've used the same ones. I remember Willie Fay, who was with Popular Publications and went on to Hollywood. He had the same short story that he sold year after year to both the SATURDAY EVENING POST and COLLIER'S, about the aging athlete. In fall, he had the aging football player, and in summer, the aging baseball player. Now and then he would have an aging prize fighter. But you become aware that you've sold this story before, and if you're acutely aware of it, it hurts the spontaneity.

"I wrote short stories all those years. Then the magazines began to fade. THE SATURDAY EVENING POST was using five short stories a week. Finally they got down to two. The same way with COLLIER'S. THE AMERICAN, which had been one of my steady slick markets, pretty well went out of business. Then I started doing nonfiction. Then I tried novels. But I didn't sell enough to keep from starving. The novels got published, and were fairly well reviewed. But they didn't sell. So I turned to juveniles. They don't sell any amount at one time, but they keep selling. I could make more, I'm sure, doing magazine work now, because the rates have gone up so high. The juveniles don't pay off right now. I've got better than 30 of them, and each one earns a little bit.

"I got into the slicks after the war. Before, I had sold maybe half a dozen stories to slick-paper magazines. In pulps, I sold practically everything I wrote. I was never one who could produce a great deal of copy. In 1938, I sold forty-eight stories, mostly novelettes. I never could quite do one a week, and that year was my best one. I wrote slowly and rewrote as I went. Each time I stopped for lunch, I went back and read what I had written, and made pencil changes, or threw it away and started over. Of course, by the time I had finished the story, I had been over it sixteen or eighteen times. I wrote faster at first than I did as time went on. For the slicks, I might work on something all day and wind up with three hundred words less than I had the day before. I typed my own stories. But when I got through with a page, it was written up and down and on the sides, on the back, with fragments to insert here and there. A story of ten pages would probably have thirty pages of notes and additions. My wife retyped all my stories. The only reason I could work slowly in the pulps and get by was that during the Depression it didn't take much to live on. When I got married and came down here, I was making $3000 a year. We could live fairly well on that.

"As for ideas for my stories, I worked them out fairly well in my mind before I started writing. I could never do like Arthur Burks, look at a picture and then start telling a story about it. When I first started writing, I would work out just about all the details. Later, when I wrote detective stories, I would get an idea and go on from there. One thing I always wanted to know completely was the villain. It all turned on him. The hero could make mistakes in trying to find him. He could blunder. The villain knew damn well what he was doing. So you couldn't have him do something contrary to his normal actions. It got to where I would start a story without knowing how the hero was going to catch the villain.

"I remember the characters more than the plots. I liked the Bishop, in BLACK MASK. He was a peg-legged newspaper man. He was fashioned after a man I worked with on the old "Montgomery Advertiser." In fact, the only thing I changed was the name of the paper. Another character was Joe Gee, the detective who couldn't sleep while on a case. He had a very short name so you could write it without wasting any time . . . and it still counted as two words.

"I did most of my pulp work for Popular. They had a whole string of magazines. I don't think I ever got more than a cent and a half a word, and it took quite a while to get to that point. I got two cents a word from BLACK MASK. DETECTIVE FICTION WEEKLY also paid fairly well. In all my years with Popular, I never met Henry Steeger. I knew Alden Norton, Mike Tilden, Steve Fisher, Frank Gruber and Arthur Burks. Burks frequently went to work at midnight and kept at it until daylight.

"I liked to write the weird story, when I could actually use the supernatural element in it. When the weird markets began closing down, I did more and more detectives. I didn't write for WEIRD TALES, since it was only paying as I remember, about half a cent a word. If you're a slow producer, you just can't eat on that. Oh, I've sold stories as low as a quarter a cent, and stories I never got paid for. These were usually rejects that didn't make it somewhere else. But I sold most of my original markets.

"When my stories came out, I usually read them to see what the editors had done to them. They cut words and passages to make them fit; they didn't change much. The one exception was the first time I ever had my name on the cover, with the cover painting illustrating my story. I don't remember the name of the magazine. It was sold through Woolworth's. It didn't last long, and I can tell you why. I had worked real hard, and was very proud of it. The solution to the story was in the final paragraph. Well, to make it come out even at the end, instead of cutting a line here and there, the editor cut the final paragraph. I don't think he lasted very long, either."

Today, Blassingame continues with his juveniles, about four a year, plus short submissions to youth magazines. Like several other pulpsters from the thirties, who still keep their hand in writing, he finds the fact article the best way to earn a modest income. For as Wyatt Blassingame says, "Short story writing is a young man's game."

INDEX

www.ingramcontent.com/pod-product-compliance
Lightning Source LLC
Chambersburg PA
CBHW031245090426
42742CB00007B/325